THE LIVES AND LEGACY OF AN EAST TEXAS FAMILY

Joel V. Fears, Sr.

FEARS DESCENDANTS

Augustus (Gus) Fears

Augustus Fears & Roxie Burk Fears

Jonathan Turner Fears (J.T.)

Jonathan Turner Fears & Belma Denman Fears

Roxie Fears Sanders   James Denman Fears   Johnny Lee Fears

Jonathan Turner Fears, Jr.   Shirley Fears Davis   Joel Van Fears (J.V.)

FROM GEORGIA TO TEXAS

THE LIVES AND LEGACY

OF AN

EAST TEXAS FAMILY

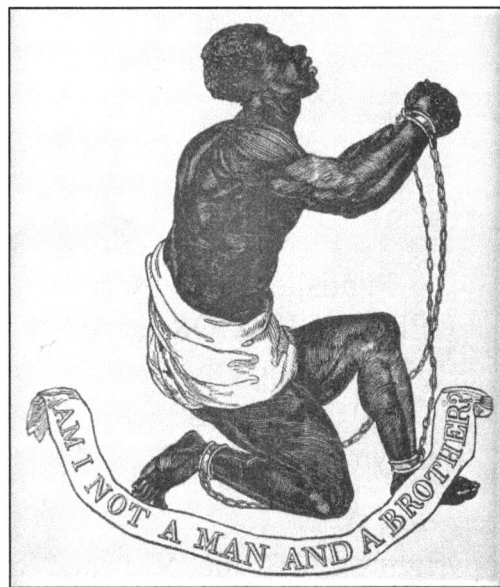

1837

FROM

SLAVERY TO FREEDOM

Fears Family History

Joel V. Fears, Sr.

HERITAGE BOOKS
AN IMPRINT OF HERITAGE BOOKS, INC.

BOOKS, CD's and more—Worldwide

For our listing of thousands of titles see our website
At
www.HeritageBooks.com

Published 2015 by
HERITAGE BOOKS, INC
Publishing Division
5810 Ruatan Street
Berwyn Heights, MD 20740

International Standard Book Numbers
Paperbound: 978-0-7884-5650-3
Clothbound: 978-0-7884-6186-6

DEDICATION

Many people sacrificed much with hard work, prayers, faith and determination, which brought the Fears family to the present day. Therefore, it is with thankfulness to them, to God who blessed them for their faithfulness and to the many hundreds gone that this story is dedicated.

FOREWORD

SLAVERY IN AMERICA

"The enslavement of blacks in the American Colonies began during the 1600's. Slavery flourished in the South where large plantations grew cotton, tobacco, and other crops. The plantations required large numbers of laborers.

By 1860, the slave states had about 4 million slaves. The slaves made up nearly a third of the South's population."   World Book Encyclopedia, Volume 17, 1991, pg. 504

Within the 4 million slaves in the United States in 1860, were the great-grandparents and grandparents of the author of this book, Joel V. Fears, Sr. Beginning with them, the story of the Fears family is written.

x

ACKNOWLEDGMENTS

Grateful acknowledgment is given to those who patiently awaited the publishing of this book promised years before. Church responsibilities, Civil War reenactments, travel and helping others, were the walls that I had to overcome until, with my wife's insistence, I set my face to it's completion. Information for completing this book came from many sources: archives, libraries, relatives, young and old, and from locations such as: Nacogdoches, Texas; Lufkin Texas; San Antonio, Texas; Atlanta, Georgia and Washington, D.C. However, I was most influenced by the many family stories told by my father, Jonathan T. Fears, Sr. as we sat on the front porch of our house. It was a ritual that followed after supper for enjoying the cool of the evening. *Lives and Legacy of an East Texas Family* is a work that I am hopeful that this present family generation and generations to come will remember, and appreciate the miles that our family had to go and the bridges over challenges that they had to cross. Read, enjoy, remember and pass on.

CONTENTS

xiii

INTRODUCTION

I recall with fond memories the stories my father, Jonathan Turner Fears or "J. T." so called by those who knew him, vividly told of relatives far and near, living and long departed. I heard stories about his family's growing up in Nacogdoches, Appleby, Caro and Trawick, about World War I, and many other places, peoples, and events in Nacogdoches County and around Eastern Texas. Unless we pass along these treasured stories and consciously dig into our past, our knowledge of our ancestors will grow dim and become lost to our descendants. I, therefore, from my years of family genealogical research, will share the joy of discoveries and invite readers to join me in finding and preserving the precious memories of our ancestors. There is joy in finding and preserving those memories and in ensuring that our ancestors are never forgotten and that their names will always be spoken.

The following is an excerpt from Dr. James Dobson's book, *Home With a Heart*, which appeared in the March 1997 issue of *Focus on the Family Magazine*:
"Preserving Your Family Heritage"

The lyrics of an African folk song say that when an old person dies, it's as if a library has burned down. It is true. There's a richness of family heritage in each person's life that will be lost if it isn't passed on to the next generation.

To preserve this heritage for our children, we must tell them where we've been and how we got to this moment. Sharing about our faith, our early family experiences, the obstacles we overcame or the failures we suffered can bring a family together and give it a sense of identity.

The stories of one's past, and childhood, also the courtship with one's spouse, etc., can be treasures to his or her children. Unless those experiences are shared with them, that part of their history will be gone forever. Every one should take the time to make yesterday come alive for the children in each family.

"What became of the people of Sumer?" the traveler asked the old man, "for ancient records show that the people of Sumer were Black." "What happened to them?" "Ah", the old man sighed. "They lost their history, so they died." It is with these prophetic words that we begin our journey through history.

Joel Van Fears, Sr.

Chapter One
OUR ROOTS

"We can chart our future clearly and wisely only when we know the path which has led to the present." Adlai E. Stevenson

The journey into the future begins with a look back in time to our oldest confirmed ancestor on the Fears side of the family. Jonathan Turner (J. T.) Fears, Sr. often spoke to his children of his grandmother Beedie's (Bedy) story about being brought from Georgia as a slave and that a sister was left in Georgia. However, her sister's name was not passed down. J. T. said that his father, Gus spoke of Macon and Atlanta, Georgia, although he might have been too young to remember being in Georgia. Later discoveries of records enabled the determination of Beedie's place of origin in Georgia and approximate time of transfer to Texas, primarily through location of records in the Stephen F. Austin College Library in Nacogdoches, Texas. But, first found was information from the 1850 Georgia Census Index, during a visit to the Macon County Library in Macon, Georgia by Joel Fears. Found was the location of the white Fears in Georgia counties. They were located in five Georgia counties: Henry, Jasper, Morgan, Harris, and Troup.

Census Index, 1850 Georgia

NAME	COUNTY	PAGE#	LOCATION
FEARS, A. B.	Henry	213	42nd Dist.
FEARS, Ezekiel	Jasper	087	46 Dist
FEARS, Ezekiel P.	Jasper	116	46 Dist
FEARS, Henry C.	Morgan	104	62nd Dist
FEARS, James	Morgan	103	62nd Dist
FEARS, John H.	Morgan	103	62nd Dist
FEARS, John P.	Jasper	128	46th Dist
FEARS, Josephine	Harris	093	19th Dist
FEARS, Nancy	Harris	085	Gooding
FEARS, Oliver P.	Troup	126	655 Dist.
FEARS, P. T.	Henry	237	47th Dist.
FEARS, Riley	Jasper	117	46th Dist
FEARS, Thomas	Henry	208	42 Dist.
FEARS, Thomas J.	Harris	124	Osborne
FEARS, W. S.	Henry	239	42nd Dist.
FEARS, Wiley M.	Henry	190	42nd Dist.
FEARS, Zachariah	Morgan	103	62nd Dist.

Learned from J. T. Fears was that Dr. "Porter" Fears (William Porter Fears) son of Oliver P. Fears was their family doctor and Dr. Fears' visits to his home. Later found was evidence that Dr. William Porter Fears lived and practiced medicine in Appleby, Texas where J. T. Fears was born. From this information, was known the state and the name to look for. Although Fears' were located in several counties in Georgia in the 1850 Census Index, most revealing was a discovery in the Lufkin, Texas library genealogy section. Those Georgia locations of interest were Troup and Coweta Counties. Oliver P. Fears had lived in both counties.

Name	Relationship	Color	Sex	Age	Birthplace	Occupation
Oliver P. Fears	Head	White	Male	43	Georgia	Planter
Sarah A.	Wife	White	Female	25	Georgia	
William P.	Son	White	Male	5	Georgia	
John B.	Son	White	Male	4	Georgia	
Henry L.	Son	White	Male	3	Georgia	
Susan L.	Daughter	White	Female	1	Georgia	

Extract From 1850 Georgia Census - Coweta County 655th Dist., page 251

Additional evidence revealed that Oliver Porter was the owner of a business in Coweta County Georgia. Mary Jackson Fears, Joel's wife, directed him to a book, Coweta County Chronicles for One Hundred Years, in the Kurth Memorial Library, Lufkin, Texas. Found in that book was that Oliver Porter had bought a dry goods store in the town of Newnan, which he later sold before moving to Texas in 1859.

REMOVAL. "The subscriber would respectfully inform his friends and the public generally that he has removed his stock of Dry Goods to the large and commodus Store House situated on the North East corner of the public square formerly occupied by Hilley & Alexander, where he is receiving and opening one of the largest and best selected stocks of DRY GOODS ever offered in Western Georgia. O. P. FEARS."

From Jones, Mary G and Lily Reynolds, *Coweta County Chronicles for One Hundred Years,* p.126, Stern Printing Co., Atlanta, Ga. 1928.

Another book, *A* History of Coweta County..., provided information about the closing of Oliver's business. *"1859 - Mr. P. Fears, a merchant, closed his business and Mr. Herrin sold out and moved to Texas, and other changes."* W. U. Anderson, A History of Coweta County From 1825 To 1880. This was the first confirmation of the Fears' link to Georgia and an approximate date when our ancestor Beedie, her son Gus (Augustus) and Gus's sister Caroline (Callie) with other slaves of Oliver Porter Fears and his wife, Sarah Ann Battle Long Fears were brought to Texas. Additional confirmation was obtained from a book in the Lufkin, Texas library, Texas and Texans that gave information about Dr. John B. Fears, the second son of Oliver Porter Fears.

John B. Fears

Dr. Fears is a native of Troup County Georgia and was born November 17, 1844. He was reared in Coweta County and received his early education in Newnan and accompanied his parents by water to Shreveport from Mobile to Montgomery County Alabama. He then came by private conveyance to Nacogdoches County in the fall of 1859. His father died in 1885 at the age of 77. He was Oliver Porter Fears, who in 1851 and 1852 had been a merchant in Atlanta, Georgia. In 1853, he moved to Newnan and there carried on merchants business until coming to Texas in 1859.

Dr. Fears' mother was Sarah Ann Battle Long, a daughter of Col. Henry Long, of Troup Co. Georgia. Colonel Long was a farmer on a large scale and large slaveholder and gave his influence to the Confederacy in the army of which he had four sons. Oliver P. and Sarah Ann Fears were the parents of the following children: Dr. William P. a physician of Appleby, Texas, John B. Fears, Susan Long, Mary Emma, Rebecca, and Watson.

Johnson, John B. Fears, Vol. III of A History of Texas and Texans, (The American Historical Society, 1914) 1407 - 08.

In July of 1994, was experienced the happy and emotional discovery at the Ralph Steen Library of a copy of the actual deed of gift transferring ownership of these poor souls from Col. Henry Long, Sarah Ann's Father, to her with her husband Oliver as trustee. Other slaves Oliver and Sarah inherited from his father and her father were also brought to Texas and also retained the Fears surname. Now confirmed was the link of the slaveholder to Georgia, the approximate time of their relocation to Texas and finally that they were in fact, the slaveholders of our ancestors. However, more discoveries were to follow. This was only part of the story of the odyssey of our ancestors.

State of Georgia | Known all men by these present that I Henry Long of
County of Troup |
the state and county aforesaid for and in consideration of the sum
of Five Dollars cash in hand to me paid as well as in consideration
of the natural love regard and affection I have and bear towards
my daughter Sarah Ann Battle Fears and her children now living and
which may hereafter be born hath given granted aliened & conveyed
and doth by these presents give grant alien and convey unto my said
daughter Sarah A.B. Fears and her children now living and which may
hereafter be born, the following property towit, Lewis a man aged about (67)
sixty seven years of dark complexion; Job a man aged about (30) thirty years
of dark complexion; Anderson a boy aged about (16) Sixteen years of copper
Complexion; Winny a woman aged about (30) thirty years of dark complexion
<u>Bidy</u> a woman aged about (22) twenty-two years of dark complexion. Betsy
a girl aged about (11) Eleven years of copper complexion. Ellen a girl aged
about (5) five years mulatto. <u>Gus</u> a boy aged about (3) three years a mulatto,
<u>Caroline</u> a girl about (1 1/2) one and one-half years old to and for her and
their only sole and separate use forever free from the debt liabilities and
control of her present or of any future husband her interest therein to
constitute her separate Estate to be for her exclusive use & benefit to have
and to hold the said property to her & them forever limited to their use
as above set forth. In testimony where of I have here unto set my hand and
affixed my sea this the fifth day of November A.D. 1859.
Signed sealed & delivered in presence of
R.A. T. Ridley   Henry Long   {Seal}
Benj. H. Bigham
     Notary public
           Recorded Nov 8th 1859
                Wm M. Latimer   Clk

Deed - Henry Long to Sarah A. B. Fears

During a trip to Troup County Georgia, the next important discovery occurred.

At the LaGrange Archives the original deed book was found in which was recorded the original deed of gift that transferred our ancestors from Col. Long to his daughter. But a more interesting discovery was that of a deed of gift that first transferred them to Col. Long from Dr. William Beasley. Therefore, I concluded that the transfer was from Beasley to Long and from Long to his daughter Sarah Ann Battle Long Fears. How and when Dr. Beasley acquired Beedie, Caroline and Gus was not determined.

On November 5, 1859, William P. Beasley sold for "five dollars the following property to wit: Lewis a man aged about 67 yrs. of dark complexion, Job a man aged about 30 years of dark complexion, Anderson, a boy aged about 16 yrs. of copper complexion, Winny a woman aged about 30 yrs. of dark complexion, Bidy(Beedie) a woman aged about 22 years of dark complexion, Betsey a girl aged about 11 years of copper complexion, a girl aged about 5 years mulatto, Gus a boy aged about 3 years a mulatto, Caroline, a girl about 1 1/2..." Bidy(Beedie) was the mother of Gus and his sister Caroline.

Georgia | Know all men by these presents that for and in consideration
Troup County | of five Dollars cash in hand to me paid & for divers other goods & valuable considerations me hereunto knowing, I William P. Beasley of said State and County have transferred sold and delivered & relinquish and doth by these present transfer sell deliver and relinquish to Henry Long of said County his being administrator Executor and asigns all of my rights-title and interest in and to the following property towit Lewis a man age about (67) sixty seven years of dark complexion, Job a man aged about (30) thirty years of dark complexion. Anderson a boy aged about (16) sixteen years of copper complexion. Winny a woman aged about (30) thirty years of dark complexion Bidy a woman aged about (22) twenty two years of dark complexion, Betsey a girl aged about (11) Eleven years of copper complexion, Ellen a girl aged about (5) years mulatto Gus a boy aged about (3) three years a mulatto Caroline a girl about (1 1/2) on and one half years old. So that from this time henceforth all of my interest in this property doth cease determine & vest as above. Witness my hand and seal-this 5th day of November A.D. 1859. Signed sealed and delivered in presence of
R. A. T. Ridley
Benj. H. Bigham Not. Pub.   William P. Beasley {seal}
Recorded Dec 20, 1859
WmM latimer clk

William P. Beasley to Long Deed 1859

The date of the Beasley deed was the same date, November 5, 1859, that a Deed of Gift with the same wording was recorded for Col. Henry Long giving the same slave property to his daughter, Sarah Ann Battle Fears for five dollars in "consideration of the natural love, regard and affection." Sarah Ann Battle Fears traveled with her husband, William Porter Fears, a merchant, and her "gift" property (slaves) "by boat to New Orleans and by private conveyance into Nacogdoches County, Texas." Beedie/Bidy, Gus and Caroline, taken from their Georgia kin and with their new master and mistress, came to live in Nacogdoches County, Texas.

These two records, one from Stephen F. Austin State University, Ralph W. Steen Library, Nacogdoches, Texas and the other from Troup County Archives, LaGrange, Georgia revealed how the Fears family from Troup County, Georgia became Texans.

Joel and wife Mary decided on a visit to Georgia to meet the descendants of the slaveholders of Mary's ancestors, the McCants in Butler, Georgia and afterwards visit the Georgia Archives. It was an interesting experience to see the land, the graves of slaveholders and slaves, and the few remaining structures as well as the visit with the slaveholder's descendants. They were well received and were given a tour of the vast land holdings of the McCants descendants. It was on this trip that the documented facts were discovered as to how Dr. Beasley had acquired Beady, Gus and his sister Caroline.

At this point of research, the thought for certain was that it was known how Oliver Porter Fears had acquired The Fears' slave ancestors. However, this trip to Georgia was to instill in the researcher the knowledge that there are no absolutes in slave ancestral research. Each new discovery creates more questions and we are off searching again. An 1856 Sheriff's sale in Coweta County Georgia was to prove this point.

1856 - A deed found recorded in the Coweta County Court House recorded that The Bank of Georgia had foreclosed on the debt owed by Oliver Porter Fears and had put up for auction, property which included Beedie and Gus, along with other slaves as payment for the debt.

Entering into this drama was Henry Long, Oliver's father-in-law and Henry's friend and business partner Dr. William Beasley. Each had joined forces to place the highest bid for Oliver's property, thus saving him from financial ruin.

This event could have also changed the course of history for our family, a different name perhaps or some state other than Texas in which to enter freedom. However, the family was to remain intact with Oliver Porter Fears and his wife Sarah Ann Battle Fears. Hence, the need for the 1859 deeds, which returned the slave property to Oliver's wife prior to the family's move to Texas, was determined. The question again is asked. Where and from whom did Oliver first acquire Beedie?

1856 Sheriff's sale (Coweta Co.)

James L. Calhoun		State of Georgia County of Coweta
Sheriff of Coweta County		I Whereas heretofore towit on the 30th Thirthieth day
To		I of January in the year Eighteen Hundred
Henry Long &		I and fifty Six I James L Calhoun Sheriff of
William P. Beasley	I said county of Coweta did seize the property
_____		I real and personal herein after described as the

property of Oliver P. Fears under and virture of a fiari frairs in??? from the Superior court of said county of Coweta in favor of the Bank of the State of Georgia against said Oliver P. Fears as maker and Henry Long and William P. Beasley as indensers for the principal debt of two thousand dollars besides interest and costs and whereas after said property was duly advertised as required by law the same in proper parcels was duly exposed to sale before the court house door in said county on this day being the first Sunday in March and during the legal hour of sale and after the same was duly cried was duly knocked off to Henry Long and William P. Beasley as the highest and best bidders therefore and which highest bid amount to the sum of Eight thousand seven hundred and eighty dollars. Now therefore for and in consideration of the promises and for and in consideration of the said sum of Eight thousand Seven Hundred and eighty dollars cash in hand paid by the said Henry Long and William P. Beasley at and before the sealing and delivery of these presents the receipt whereof is hereby acknowledged this indenture witnesseth by the said James L. Calhoun as Sheriff of said county have granted bargained sell and conveyed and with these present grant bargain sell and convey unto the said Henry Long and William P. Beasley their heirs and aligned by virtue of the promised and by virtue of my office as Sheriff as aforesaid the following property towit one dwelling house and lot in the town of Newnan in said county wherein Oliver P. Fears now lives on Greenville Street and adjourning the lots of Henry Keller King, King W. Perry and Joseph G. Brow and one hundred acres of land known as West half of lot No. (28) twenty eight in the second district of said county of Coweta and the following slaves towit Lewis a man about fifty years of age Ben a man about twenty four years of age, Job a man about twenty four years of age, Louisa a woman about twenty years of age, Patience a woman about fifty years of age, Anderson a boy about nine years of age, Betty a girl about eight years of age, Biddy a woman about eighteen years of age and her child one year old Winny a woman about twenty four years of age, Nathan a man about thirty two years of age and Creasy a woman about thirty years of age, all of which property was pointed out by said Oliver P. Fears to have and to hold unto them the said Henry Long and William P. Beasley their heirs and assigns the said described property the appertainances and the increase to them and their own proper use benefit and behoof forever in the simple and all the wright title interest and claim of the said Oliver P. Fears his heirs Executors and administrators in and for said property by virtue of the promises and as Sheriff as aforesaid and as far as the law doth authorize in said cases I convey to the said Henry Long and William P. Beasley their heirs executors administrators and assigns. In witness of all which I have hereby set my hand and officers seal this the 4th day of March 1856 in presence of us as witness   IB. H. Hill   I James L. Calhoun Sheriff
Asa Huggins J,   IRecorded this March 20

1856 Sheriff Sale

7

Following the 1856 foreclosure, an 1857 tax record for Oliver Fears showed that he was now an agent for Henry Long and William Beasley with the land and 9 slaves valued at $7,300, two less than recorded at the Sheriff's sale. Oliver and Sarah were recorded as having the three slaves given to them by James Fears for which they were taxed at an estimated value of $1,600. The aggregate value of all property was $9,452. This was far less than the total value of $15,987 listed for taxing in 1850 and 1851, which included 19 slaves.

In 1858, Henry Long deeded two additional slaves, Amelia and Amanda (her child) to his daughter Sarah. To protect their wealth, most of their valuable property; primarily their slaves, Oliver and Sarah had allowed ownership to be given to Sarah.

1858

State of Georgia Troup County.

     Whereas heretofore towit on the 20th day of December 1858 I delivered to my daughter hereinafter named the negroes named on the terms herein specified to her and her children in the presence of Thomas B. Greenwood, Edmund S. Harris and Albert E. Cox being said and understood that the gift was to be reduced to writing as herein after set forth: Now therefore in consideration of the promises, and for the natural love and affection which I bear for my daughter Sarah A. B. Fears: and for other considerations I have given and conveyed and by these presents do give and convey to Oliver P. Fears as trustee for the sole and separate use of said Sarah A. B. Fears during her life the following negroes towit: Amelia a woman, and her child Amanda a girl and all their increase since the 20th day of December last. I have not a son To hold and use for the of said Sarah A. B. Fears during her life and then to her children equally. On

Signed sealed and delivered in presence of |

 Thos. B Greenwood | Henry Long {Seal}

 Albert E. Alex |

                    Recorded 13th May 1859

                            Wm M. Latimer Clk.

1859 Deed: Long To Sarah A. B. Fears

1859 Deed: Long To Sarah A. B. Fears

Also assisting in restoring the wealth of Oliver Fears and his wife Sarah was James Fears, the father of Oliver. James by deed of gift transferred three slaves to Sarah by way of Oliver as trustee.

1856 James Fears	Georgia Morgain County
To	This Indenture made and entered into this day 27th day of
Oliver P. Fears	December Eighteen hundred and fifty six between James

Fears of the county and state first aforesaid of the one part and Oliver P. Fears of the county of Coweta and said state of the other part witnesseth that for and in consideration of the love and affection which he the said James Fears has and bear to his daugthter in law Sarah Ann Fears wife of the said Oliver P. Fears and his grand children the children of said Oliver P. Fears and for and in consideration of five Dollars cash in hand paid by the said Oliver P. Fears at and before the sealin and delivery of these presents the receipt whereof is hereby acknowledged and for the purpose of providing a suitable maintenance for the said Sarah Ann Fears and the children she now has and those she may hereafter have by her present husband the said Oliver P. Fears during her life and for the purpose of providing for said children a portion after the death of the said Sarah Ann Fears he the said James Fears hath bargained sold and conveyed and doth by these present bargain sell and conveyed unto the said Oliver P. Fears as trustee in trust for the sole and Negroes use benefit and advantage of the said Sarah Ann Fears and all her said children by her present husband the said the Oliver P. Fears during the natural life of the said Sarah Ann Fears free and exempt from all the debts liabilities and contracts present and future of her present or any future husband and exempt from the mantal rights control or disposition of her present or any future husband and in the decrease of the said Sarah Ann Fears for the use and benefit of and to be equally divided among all of her said children by her present husband that may be living at the time of her death the following named and described `Negroes to wit. Seaborn a man Twenty-two years of age Nicey Ann a girl Nineteen years of age and Joullious a boy Two years of age. To have and to hold the above described Negroes and their increase unto him the said Oliver P. Fears as trustee as aforesaid for the sole and Negroes use benefit and advantage of the said Sarah Ann Fears and the children she now has and those she may hereafter have by the present husband the said Oliver P. Fears during the Natural life of the said Sarah Ann Fears free and exempt from all the debts liabilities and contracts Present and future of the present or any future husband and free and exempt from the mantal rights control or dispostion of her present or any future husband and on the decease of the said Sarah Ann Fears to have and to hold the said 26 Negroes as trusetee as aforesaid in trust for the use and benefit of and to be equally divided among all the aforesaid children of the said Sarah Ann Fears by the said present husband that may be living at the time of her death and the said Oliver P. Fears if he shall at any time hereafter during the life of the said Sarah Ann Fears deem it advantageous to the interest of the said Sarah Ann and her children aforesaid to modify and change the species of property hereby conveyed is hereby authorized and empowered as trustee as aforesaid and for the use and towit aforesaid by and with the consent and apputation of the said Sarah Ann to sell my one or more of said Negroes and the proceeds of the sale thereof to invest in Rail Road Stock, Bank Stock or any other species of said Rail Road Stock, Bank Stock or other species of property as Trustee as aforesaid to hold for the use & benefit of the said Sarah Ann and her said children upon ?? Trusts and subject to the same conditions and limitations on every subject as are herein and hereby limited and declared intended to be limited and declared of and in the Negroes herein and hereby conveyed. In witness whereof the said James Fears has hereunto set his hand and affixed his seal the day and year above written.

Signed Sealed and delivered} in presence of

}   James Fears   {Seal} Gest Zachariah Fears}   Recorded Decr 29th 1856 Thos J. Burney J.I.C   }

M^k ? Hurkins   Clk

1856 Deed – James to Sarah A. B. Fears

The foreclosure and Sheriff's sale of 1856 precipitated Oliver and Sarah's ultimate move to Texas. Learned from other sources was the fact that this was not unique to Oliver and Sarah. Many slaveholders moved west. This was a course taken by many during the 1850's to escape creditors, efforts of Northern Abolitionist to end slavery and southern threats to go to war to preserve it. History was to prove that these tactics did not prevent the inevitable loss of slaves and property, not counting the extensive loss of American lives, both North and South and Black and White.

Dr. Fears is a native of Troup county Georgia, and was born November 17, 1844. He was reared in Coweta County, that state, received his early education at Newnan, and accompanied his parents by water to Shreveport from Mobile and to Mobile from Montgomery County, Alabama. He then came by the Morgan line of boats to New Orleans and by private conveyance to Nacogdoches County, reaching here in the fall of 1859 and engaging in farming some two and one-half miles from where the town of Garrison now stands.

Johnson, John B. Fears, Vol. III of A History of Texas and Texans, (The American Historical Society, 1914) 1407 - 08.

Many critical events preceded the arrival in Texas. The earliest identification of Beedie and her children was in the 1856 Sheriff's sale. Although these were events over which they had absolutely no control, these events affected their lives and those of generations to come. Being auctioned and sold as someone's personal property, exchanged from slaveholder to slaveholder, separation from relatives and loved ones never to see them again, and traveling to a distant land where all are strangers except those with whom you have traveled makes for a life that could only be described by those who have endured the cruel system of chattel slavery.

Who were those taken from Georgia to this strange land? The 1860 slave schedule of Nacogdoches County did not reveal much. Fifteen slaves were listed, 8 males and 7 females with their ages, color, mental condition and gender the only identifying characteristics. Who among those listed were Beedie, Gus and Caroline? Although the Slave Census' lack of key identifying information made it near impossible to identify one slave from another, their names and descriptions could possibly be matched with the Georgia deeds.

Slave Identified on deeds beginning in 1856 (14 slaves)

1856 Deed- 3 slaves (see page 10)	1859 Deed - 2 slaves (see page 9)
James Fears to Sarah Ann Fears:	Henry Long to Sarah Ann Fears:
Seaborn a man 22 years of age	Amelia a woman and her child Amanda
Nicey Ann a girl 19 of age	
Joullious a boy 2 years of age	

1859 Deed - 9 slaves (see page 9)
Henry Long to Sarah Ann Fears:

Lewis a man aged about 67   Betsey a girl aged about 11
Job a man aged about 30   Ellen a girl aged about 5 years
Anderson a boy aged about 16   Gus a boy aged about 3
Winney a woman aged about 30   Caroline a girl $1\frac{1}{2}$
Bidy a woman aged about 22

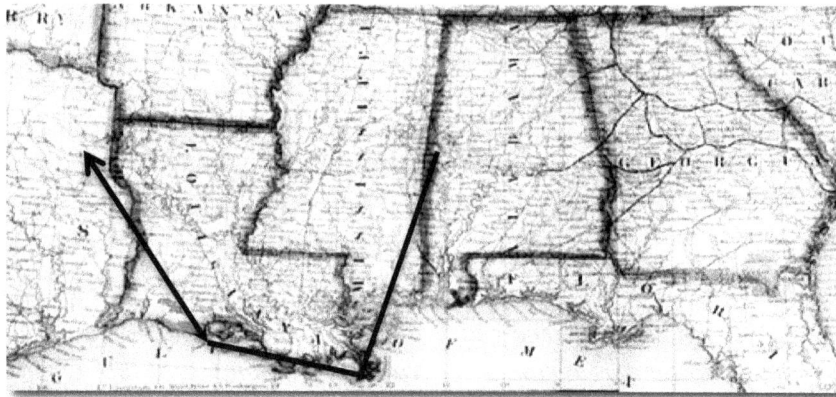

From Georgia To Texas

The fourteen listed previously are one less than the count of slaves on the 1860 schedule. The difference cannot be accurately accounted for. However, the one-year-old male slave child could have been born in Texas. Beedie's husband, Tom Fears was not identified on any of the Georgia slave list, although the 1870 Nacogdoches County Census recorded that he was born in Georgia. Could this also account for the difference? How many were left in Georgia and which ones were brought to Texas cannot be determined with certainty except for those later identified through Texas census records.

Names of Slave Owner	No. Slaves	Age	Sex	Color
Oliver P. Fears	1	30	F	B
	1	24	F	B
	1	24	F	B
	1	21	F	B
	1	14	F	B
	1	6	F	B
	1	5	F	B
	1	4	M	B
	1	2	M	B
	1	1	M	B
Oliver P. Fears	1	65	M	B
	1	28	M	B
	1	24	M	B
	1	24	M	B
	1	18	M	M

1860 Slave Schedule

Assessment of Property, situated in the County, for 1860					
Negroes		Horses		Cattle	
No.	Value	No.	Value	No.	Value
9	5650				
4	2900	2	400		

1860 Property Assessment of Nacogdoches Co. Listed in addition to other property,

13 taxable slaves.

THE AMERICAN CIVIL WAR

Lincoln became the 16th President of the United States mainly from the votes coming from the north. Lincoln was an opponent of slavery. The south made it known that this was going to split the United States if Lincoln were elected. Therefore, on December 20, 1860, secession took place with South Carolina taking the lead, followed in January 1861, by the states of Alabama, Florida, Georgia, Louisiana, and Mississippi. They formed a separate Union within the United States called the Confederate States of America. Before the end of February, five other states joined the Confederacy. They were Arkansas, North Carolina, Tennessee, Texas, and Virginia.

When Abraham Lincoln took office on March 4, 1861 - the United States was a divided country with slavery as the major issue before the Republic.

The South moved fast and decided to seize U.S. Federal forts within their jurisdiction. Fort Sumter in Charleston Harbor was considered a Union stronghold. Lincoln provided stronger protection for Fort Sumter. Therefore, it had to be taken by force by the Confederates. The firing on Fort Sumter on April 12, 1861 was the start of the American Civil War. Abraham Lincoln had been in office only one month. The Civil War began in South Carolina soon after the occupation of the Federal Fort Sumter and the state's secession from the Union in 1861. Long Island University, C.W. Post Campus website:

The African American: A Journey from Slavery to Freedom,

(www.cwpost.liunet.edu/cwis/cwp/library/aaslavry.htm).

The inevitable end of slavery with the victory of the Union Army was realized in Texas on June 19, 1865 when the Union Army landed at Galveston, where Major General Gordon Granger issued General Order No. 3 ending slavery in the last state of the former Confederacy.

General Order No. 3

"The people of Texas are informed that in accordance with a Proclamation from the Executive of the United States, all slaves are free. This involves an absolute equality of rights and rights of property between former masters and slaves, and the connection heretofore existing between them becomes that between employer and free laborer."

Note: The author's grandmother Roxie was a child on Galveston Island when the Union Army landed.

Between the end of the Civil War that brought freedom on June 19, 1865 after the arrival of General Gordon Granger at Galveston and the first census in 1870, some of the freedmen probably left the county or took a surname other than Fears. However, Beedie, her husband and other freedmen chose to remain in the area in which they were once slaves of Oliver P. and Sarah A. B. Fears.

What was life like after slavery for Beedie and her descendants?

The 1867 poll list of Freedmen was the first official record found that listed Tom Fears and Seaborn (Ceburn), each listed as paying $1.00 state tax and $0.50 county tax. In 1868 another tax list shows Tom and Seaborn as owners of property. Property taxes and voting are facts of life that, even to this day, establish an individual as being a citizen of the county, state or nation. Then she or he is a resident. These men who once were slaves, listed as property on Oliver Porter Fears' Tax list in 1860, are now, seven years later, free and paying taxes on their property.

Personal Property	State Tax	Incomes and Salaries	County Tax
Name		State	County
Fears, Sebron		1.00	0.57
Fears, Tom		1.00	0.57
Sutphen, Abe		1.00	0.50

Poll List For Freedmen

BEEDIE LONG FEARS
b. Circa 1836-38
p. Georgia
d. January 17, 1925
p. Nacogdoches (Nacogdoches) Texas

Ida B., a daughter of Tom Fears and Beedie, the informant shown on Beedie's death certificate, indicated that Beedie's father was Will Long. From records found, Beedie was born about 1836-38. No additional records have been found to confirm who her father was or to show when or where he lived. However, her father could have been a slave of Col. Henry Long, the father of slaveholder Sarah Fears. No certain evidence has been found of Beedie's mother or of her sister that J. T. Fears said she often spoke of. Found in the 1870 Census of Coweta County Georgia was a woman named Beady (Beedie) Fears, age 78, listed with Rich Edmondson age 23 and his wife Louisa age 20. The relationship was not indicated. Could they have been the mother and sister of Beedie Fears? The search will continue.

It appears that in Texas, Beedie used surnames other than Long and Fears. Three acres of land were deeded to Beedie Weaver by Robert W. Prion, September 1, 1879 for faithful service to his family as a servant (Book 5, p.96, Nacogdoches County Clerk). This same land was later sold in Smith County to J. E. Mayfield for $30.00 by *Bedie Fears alias Beadie Weaver*. Within the deed she was referred to as being *otherwise known as Beedie Thorn*. This is possibly an error made by the clerk. However, the deed was also co-signed by Ceburn Fears. Ceburn (Seaborn) was a slave of James Fears, father of Oliver Porter Fears who transferred Ceburn to Oliver in 1856 in Morgan County Georgia and with Beedie and others, was brought to Texas. An affidavit following the deed refers to Beedie as the wife of Ceburn. This is also a possible error because Beedie was married to Tom Fears. Ceburn or "Ceb" as he was called according to J. T, Fears, might have accompanied Beedie instead of Tom because, according to J.T. (Jonathan Turner Fears), Beedie's Grandson, only one of them could read. However, Tom was a "minister of the Gospel" as was indicated on Marriage licenses of that period.

Jonathan Fears would sometimes entertain his family by amusingly imitating Tom and Ceburn's efforts to read, with Beedie adding her comments to the effort. Tom would demonstrate his halting effort to read. Beedie would admonish Ceburn. "Ceb, You old fool, see, Tom can read." For ex-slaves who were once forbidden to read or write, learning to read was an exercise of freedom. Jonathan's (J.T.) children were continually amused by his stories of "the old days."

The Nacogdoches Co. 1870 Census shows Beedie (Beda), age 31, and Tom Fears married and living with them, in addition to Gus and Callie (Caroline), were Wiley(Wily), Doc and Ida B (Ider B). The latter three were born in Texas.

Names	Age	Sex	Color	Occupation	Value of real estate	Value of Personl Prop	Birthplace
Fears, Thomas	25	M	B	Farmer		100	Georgia
Beda	31	F	B	Keeping house			Georgia
Gus C	13	M	B				Georgia
Caroline	12	F	B				Georgia
Wily	6	M	B				Texas
Doc	3	M	B				Texas
Ider B	8/12	F	B				Texas

1870 Census - Nacogdoches County Texas

The period between 1865 and 1870 was a critical time of adjustment to freedom for the freedmen. How did Tom and Beedie manage the adjustment? Their first child, Wiley, age 6 on the 1870 Census, was apparently born the last year of slavery, followed by two additional children by 1870. What was the relationship between these freedmen and the former slaveholder who lived in the same county? By 1867, black males were given the right to vote, a privilege that was taken from white men who had rebelled against the United States Federal Government. The following describes the steps needed for them to restore that right.

1867 VOTERS' REGISTRATION: The Reconstruction Act of March 13, 1867, required the commanding officer in each military district to have, before September 1, a registration of all qualified voters in each county. The lists would be used to determine who would be eligible to vote in a constitutional convention. Since persons who had held military rank of major or above, and anyone who had taken an oath as an official to support the constitution of the United States and who had subsequently become an officer in the Confederate government were deemed ineligible, a large number of Texas residents were excluded. However, this is one of the few major resources for information about black citizens of the state. The lists were prepared by county of residence and the names entered chronologically within that county division.

The 1880 census revealed that three more children were added to the family, Hattie, Noble and Money (James?). Callie (Caroline) is no longer listed with the family but is shown in a different household listed with her Husband Willis Crawford. Gus is with the family but is also with his new wife Hannah Rusk.

Name	Color	Sex	Age prior to June 1	Relation-ship to head of house	occupa-tion	Place of birth of father	placed of birth of mother
Fears, Thomas	B	M	45		Farmer	Georgia	Georgia
Beady	B	F	36	Wife	Keeping house	Georgia	Georgia
Wiley	B	M	15			Georgia	Georgia
Doc	B	M	12			Georgia	Georgia
Ida Bell	B	F	10			Georgia	Georgia
Hattie	B	F	08			Georgia	Georgia
Noble	B	M	06			Georgia	Georgia
Money	B	M	02			Georgia	Georgia
Fears, Gus	M	M	22	Laborer		Georgia	Georgia
Hanna	M	F	18	Laborer		Tenn	Tenn

1880 Census - Nacogdoches County Texas

Main Street, Nacogdoches in 1876

On Tuesday, 10 February, Captain Charles K. Phillips, noted Nacogdoches restorationist and historian, gave a presentation based on a talk given by Giles Haltom to the Nacogdoches Rotary Club in 1926. In 1926, Mr. Haltom described each of the buildings surrounding the Square, up and down Main St., Pilar St. and surrounding areas, based on his recollections of how it had been 50 years earlier, i.e., in 1876. He told about the shops, the saloons, the hotels, the churches, the homes and their occupants and relationships. Captain Phillips both generously quoted from Haltom and generously added his own comments, based on his extensive research into several of Nacogdoches' oldest and/or most important historic buildings. Presented here is the hand drawn map Chuck Phillips produced.

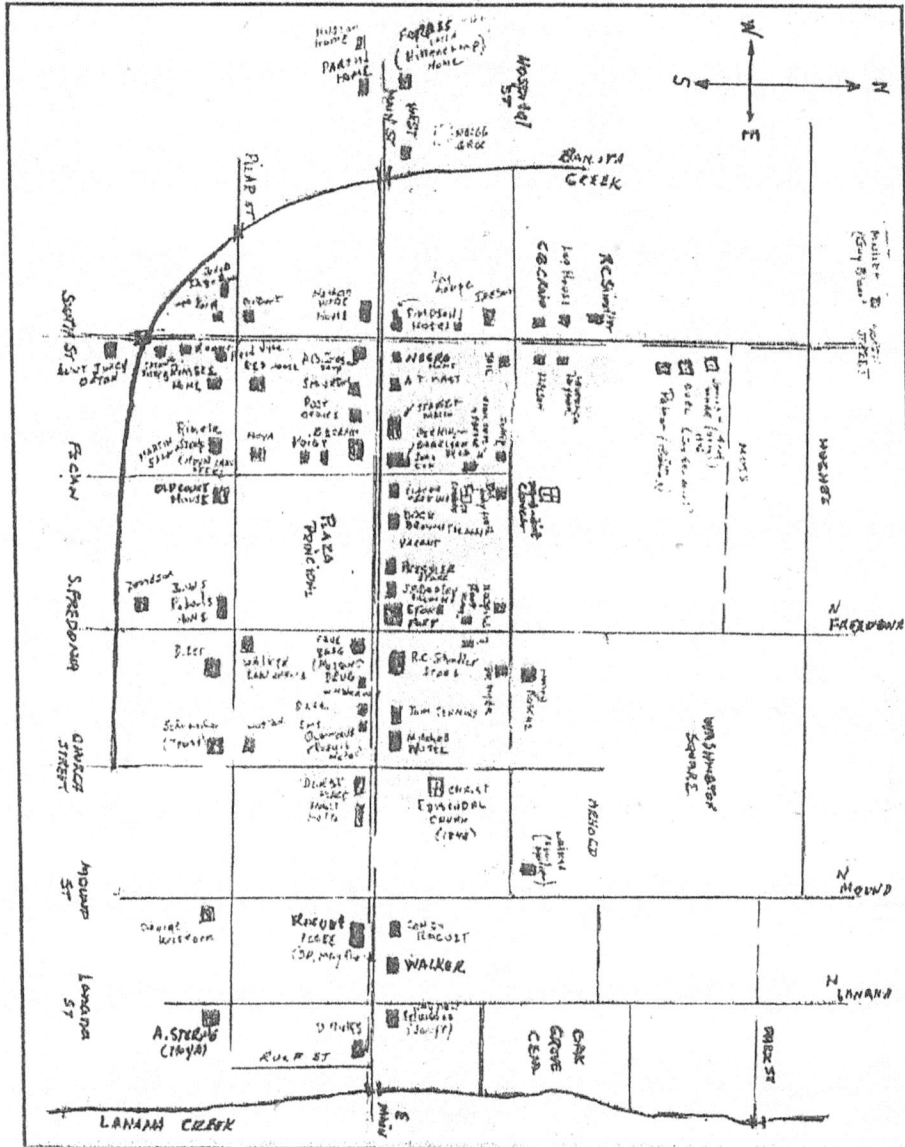

Map of Nacogdoches, 1876

There is no confirmation of any of those persons suspected of being the father of Gus and Caroline. Beedie was of dark complexion but her children Gus and Caroline were listed on the deeds as mulattos. Therefore, I believe their father could have been mulatto, Indian or White. None of Oliver Fears' adult slaves during the period of their births in Coweta County Georgia were described as mulatto, or of copper complexion.

Beedie's 1925 Death certificate

Beedie Fears, born a slave, died a free woman January 17, 1925. She is buried in the Post Oak Road cemetery, Nacogdoches, Texas. The exact location of her grave within the cemetery was not found but it might be near her son Gus' grave that was identified. Her husband, Tom Fears is possibly buried there. (See Post Oak Cemetery, pg. 25)

The following information was recorded from the Cason Monk Mortuary burial records:

Fears, Beedie   Died 17 January 1925 age 89 years
Fears, Elease   Died 28 February 1924 age 18 years
Fears, Tom,   Died 17 Feb 1912 age 83 years

BEEDIE (LONG, WEAVER) FEARS

BEEDIE (LONG, WEAVER) FEARS and UNKNOWN

1. Gus (Augustus) Fears
   b. Feb. 2, c1856   p. Coweta (County) Georgia
   d. Nov. 19, 1922   p. Caro, Texas

2. Caroline (Callie) Fears
   b. c1858   p. Coweta (County) Georgia
   d. 19??   p. Nacogdoches, Texas

Augustus (Gus) Fears
> b. circa 1855 – 57   p. Georgia
> d. Nov. 19, 1922   p. Nacogdoches (Nacogdoches) Texas
> B. Nov. 1922   p. Post Oak Cemetery

Gus is recorded as being born in 1857 in Georgia, probably in Coweta County. The 1859 Deed of gift shows his age to be about 3 years old in Troup county Georgia when he, his sister Caroline and his mother Beedie (Beady) were transferred to Sarah Ann Battle Long Fears from her father, Col. Henry Long. This indicates a birth year of 1856. However, tax records and deeds related to Oliver P. Fears indicate that Gus could have been born as early as 1855. If the 1855 date is correct, he could have, as J. T. Fears recalled, remembered dangling his feet in the waters of the Mississippi River. Gus was about eight or nine years old when the Civil War ended and slaves were actually free.

From the marriage of Gus and Hannah Rusk, his first wife, were born Emeline, Odee, Christopher, Belton, and David. Emeline, Odee and Christopher ("Lum") were the only children to survive beyond a very young age.

No | 862   xxx | State of Texas   } To any judge of the
Mr. | Gus Fears (col) | Nacogdoches Co   } County or District Court
        | To | Ordained Minister of the Gospel or Justice
Wife | Hannah Rusk (col) | of the Peace in and for said county Greetings;
        |_____| You are hereby all Authorized to solomize

the Rites of Matrimony between Mr. Gus Fears (col) and Miss Hannah

Rusk (col) and make due return to the Clerk of the County Court

of said county within sixty days thereafter, certifying

your action under this License, witness any official

signature and seal of office at office in Nacogdoches

this sixth day of December, A.D. 1879 {L.S}G. B. Crain

> Clerk Co Court Nacogdoches County

I, L. R. Hefton hereby certify that on the fourth day

of December A. D. 1879, I united in marriage Mr. Gus

Fears and Hannah Rusk the parties above named.

Witness my hand this 4th day of December A. D. 1879.

Filed January 17, 1880} Ordained Minister of the Gospel.

> G. B Crain Cenc }   M. G.

Note: In the 1900 Census of Nacogdoches County Texas (pg. 23) Gus is listed with his 2nd wife Roxy Burk.

AUGUSTUS (GUS) FEARS and HANNAH RUSK
Married December 4, 1879 in Nacogdoches, Texas

Hannah Rusk
b. abt. 1862   p. Nacogdoches (Nacogdoches) Texas
d.   p. Nacogdoches (Nacogdoches) Texas
1. Emeline
        b. 24 Oct. 1880   p. Nacogdoches (Nacogdoches) Texas
        d. 10 May 1967   p. Nacogdoches (Nacogdoches) Texas
        B. 13 May 1967   p. Nacogdoches, Texas, Pine Grove Cemetery
2. Odee
        b.   p. Nacogdoches (Nacogdoches) Texas
        d. 1 June 1959   p. Dallas, Texas
        B. 6 June 1959   p. Lincoln Memorial Cemetery Dallas, Texas
3. Christopher Columbus (Lum or C. C.)
        b. 1 July 1882   p. Nacogdoches (Nacogdoches) Texas
        d. 30 July 1954   p. Nacogdoches (Nacogdoches) Texas
        B. 1 August 1954   p. Cleaver Cemetery
4. Belton
        b.   p. Nacogdoches (Nacogdoches) Texas
        d.   p. Nacogdoches (Nacogdoches) Texas
5. David
        b.   p. Nacogdoches (Nacogdoches) Texas
        d.   p. Nacogdoches (Nacogdoches) Texas

1900 Census

Name	Relation	Race	Sex	Date of Birth	Age next	S, M, W, D	Yrs. marr.	Place of birth
Fears, Augustus	Head	B	M	1867*	33	M	18	Georgia
Roxy	Wife	B	F	1859	49	M	18	Texas
Hill, John W.	Son S.	B	M	1875	24	S		Texas
Hattie	Daughter	B	F	1882	17	S		Texas
Carrie	Daughter	B	F	1884	16	S		Texas
Mary	Daughter	B	F	1887	12	S		Texas
(*Fears*) John T.	Son	B	M	1896	4	S		Texas
(*Fears*) Bedia	Daughter	B	F	1898	1	S		Texas
(*Fears*) Columbus	Son	B	M	1882	17	S		Texas

1900 Census Nacogdoches County Texas

*Error - Should be 1857

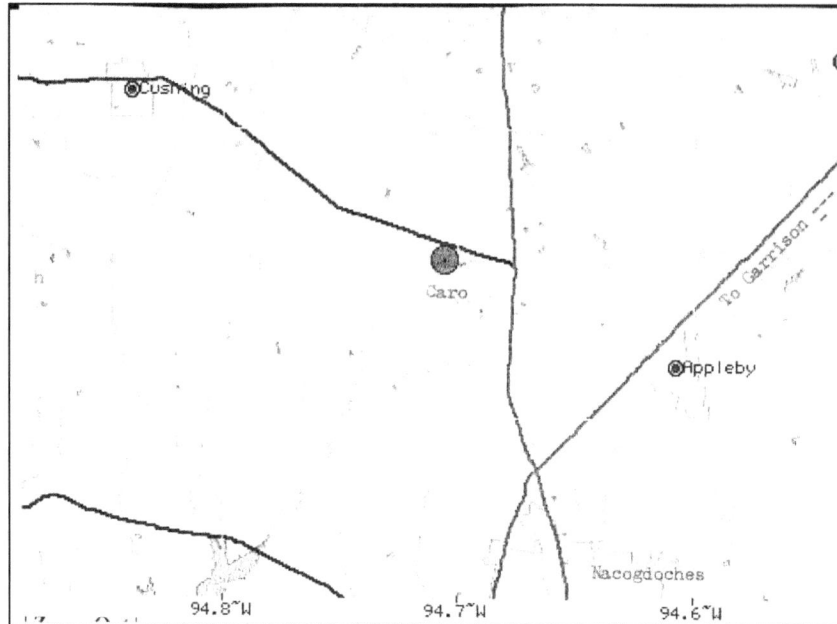

Caro Map

Gus was, according to his son Jonathan T., a very successful farmer. This was his primary occupation. He also acquired property in Caro Nacogdoches Texas as shown on deeds and maps obtained from the Nacogdoches County Court House. Caro is no longer a town. The remaining property is part of the Trawick oil lease.

Gus (Augustus) Died 19 November 1922 and is buried in the Post Oak Cemetery in Nacogdoches Texas. According to his son Jonathan, Gus died after becoming ill returning home on his horse or buggy after exposure to cold and rainy weather. Gus (Augustus) Fears, Born a slave in Georgia, died a free man in Texas.

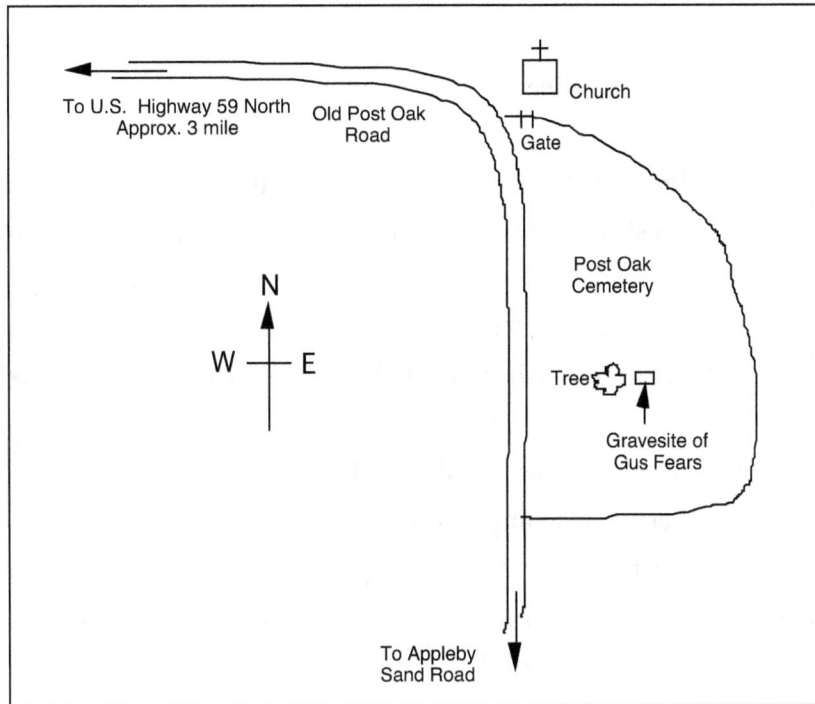

Post Oak Cemetery, Nacogdoches, Texas
Burial site of Fears freedmen and their descendants

1. Emeline

b. 24 Oct. 1880	p. Nacogdoches (Nacogdoches) Texas
d. 10 May 1967	p. Nacogdoches (Nacogdoches) Texas
B. 13 May 1967	p. Nacogdoches, Texas, Pine Grove Cemetery

Emeline Fears Carpenter

Emeline was the first child of Augustus Fears and Hannah Rusk of Post Oak community, Nacogdoches County, Texas. Her early education began in this community and later Nacogdoches Independent School District, Bishop College and Prairie View College.

Emeline was one of the early Texas educators having begun teaching around 1905 at Post Oak Community and later Nacogdoches Independent School System. It was the request of hundreds of the Nacogdoches alumni who held her in high esteem that the new Elementary School be named in her honor because of her meritorious service. She held professional membership in three organizations.

She was married to Henry Clay Carpenter of Belton, Texas. To this union were born a son who preceded her in death in infancy, and later a daughter, Helen Augusta. Emeline was active in the church, serving as president of the Missionary Circle and a member of the Deaconess Board.

Shirley Fears, Daughter of J. T. Fears, Sr. recalled how Aunt Emeline would speak to her husband the driver when they both were in the car.

Shirley said, "I would get the biggest kick out of riding with Aunt Emeline. She always called her husband Mr. Carpenter and he would say, "Leave me alone, I know what I'm doing."

Emeline Fears Carpenter – Third row left end, standing
Nacogdoches County Texas School

E. J. Campbell High School Faculty and Principal, November 1942.
Emeline Fears Carpenter is seated in front row, third from right.

HENRY CLAY CARPENTER AND EMELINE FEARS
Married 1912 in Nacogdoches, Texas

Henry Clay Carpenter
        b. 6 Oct. 1883*   p. Belton, Texas
        d. 17 February 1970   p. Marshall, Texas
        B. 21 February 1970   p Nacogdoches (Nacogdoches) Texas

Henry Clay Carpenter   Emeline Fears Carpenter

Henry Clay Carpenter was born October 6, 1883, the 14th child of Obleton and Helen
Elliott Carpenter of Belton, TX
      1. Helen
           b. 24 Oct. 19   p. Nacogdoches (Nacogdoches) Texas
           d. 26 Jun. 1999   p. Marshall, Harrison, Texas

Emeline Fears Carpenter died May 10, 1967 at the Nacogdoches City Memorial Hospital at 11:30

A.M. and was buried May 13 at the Nacogdoches Pine Grove Cemetery.

HELEN AUGUSTA CARPENTER
Teacher

b. 24 Oct. 19   p. Nacogdoches (Nacogdoches) Texas
d. June 1999   p. Marshall, Harrison, Texas
B. 26 June 1999   p. Rosehill Gardens, Marshall, Texas

Helen Augusta Carpenter was born in Nacogdoches, Texas to Henry Clay Carpenter and Emeline Fears Carpenter. She was married to the late Albert A. Sheppard on April 18, 1946. Helen married Fred Maceo Taylor, Sr. on April 9, 1989.

Helen was an honor graduate of Nacogdoches Central High School and earned her B.S. and Master's Degrees at Prairie View A&M University. She did additional studies at the University of Denver and Colorado University, Fort Collins, Colorado and Texas Women's University, Denton, Texas. Helen taught Home Economics at Burnett High School, Terrell, Texas, H. B. Pemberton High School and Marshall High School in Marshall, Texas.

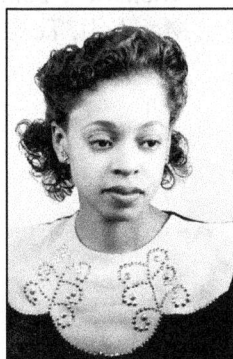

Helen Joined Zion Hill Baptist Church in Nacogdoches, Texas at an early age and served as Sunday School Teacher and Pianist for the choirs. She later joined Bethlehem Baptist Church in Terrell, Texas. After her marriage to A. L. Sheppard, the couple moved to Marshall, Texas where they joined Bethesda Baptist Church. Following the death of her husband on November 16, 1986, she was elected to serve in his stead as trustee.

Helen Fears Sheppard Taylor served as pianist of the Gospel and Senior Choirs, director and pianist of the Youth and Men's Choir, the church's Garden club, the Kitchen Planning Committee, secretary of the Trustee Board and Willing Workers Circle. She helped develop Four Seasons Estates (Fisher Drive). Helen served on the Marshall Street Committee, the Community Education Advisory Council and the Marshall Harrison County Literacy Council. She was a life member of Prairie View A & M University and Texas State Teachers Association (TSTA), Harrison County Retired Teachers Association, Vocational Advisory Council, NAACP, Mary Church Terrell Club, Marshall Community Concert Association, Marshall Regional Arts Council and Friends of the Public library. She received many awards from Future Homemakers of America, Texas Vocational Association, Marshall Independent School District and Bethesda Baptist Church.

HELEN CARPENTER AND ALBERT L. SHEPPARD
Married 18 April 1946 in Marshall, Texas

Albert L. Sheppard
    b. 20 July 1918   p. Rockwall, Texas
    d. 16 November 1986   p. Marshall, Texas
    B. 19 November 1986   p. Rosehill Gardens, Marshall, Texas

Albert L. Sheppard

Helen Carpenter Sheppard and Fred Taylor
Married April 9, 1989 In Marshall, Texas

Fred Taylor

Helen Carpenter Sheppard and Fred Taylor

Christopher Columbus "Lum" Fears, also called "C. C." was born of Augustus "Gus" Fears and Hannah Rusk. Christopher Married Hattie Hill, the daughter of his stepmother Roxie and Eli Hill. "Lum" and Hattie had two children, Eva and Rosie Lee. He later married his second wife Rebecca and Lillie, his third wife.

"Lum" also lived and worked in Keltys (Angelina) Texas and Lufkin, Angelina, Texas. He was living with his second wife Rebecca in Keltys and working at the Keltys sawmill when Jonathan Turner Fears, his half brother moved there to work at the same mill (1920-22) shortly after service in World War One in 1918 with the U.S. Army. Lum and his wife Rebecca are listed in the 1920 census of Angelina County.

Uncle Lum was a favorite uncle to all of his nieces and nephews. His visits were always greeted with delight, perhaps because of his pleasant and easygoing manner, although a gift of a nickel or dime possibly added to that delight.

The last visit to see Uncle Lum, as recalled by his nephew Joel V. Fears, was at his residence, 117 Craven St., Nacogdoches, Texas on a warm July 29 afternoon in 1954. Joel and his brother Johnny accompanied their father J.T. on a visit to their Uncle Lum who had been ill for some time. Although looking very fragile, he wanted his haircut. Joel's father, who usually did the hair cutting, asked him to do the cutting this time. He assured Uncle Lum that Joel could do it because J.V. (Joel) had often cut his hair. With a little nervousness and a little more care, unknowingly Joel had given Uncle Lum his last haircut.

Johnny was asked to remain overnight with Uncle Lum to assist him and his wife Lillie with anything that they might need. Dad and Joel returned to Lufkin. Early the next morning, July 30, at 4:30 A.M., Christopher Columbus Fears, Uncle Lum died. Uncle Lum was buried August 1, 1954 at the Cleaver Cemetery in Nacogdoches, Texas.

CHRISTOPHER COLUMBUS FEARS AND HATTIE HILL
Married in Nacogdoches, Texas

Children:
Eva
Rosa Lee

ODEE FEARS AND GILBERT RUSK
Married in Nacogdoches (Nacogdoches) Texas

GUS FEARS AND ROXIE BURK HILL

Gus (Augustus) married his second wife, Roxie Burk Hill, her second marriage, in 1893. From this union were born Jonathan Turner {J. T.) and Beedie Fitzanna. The 1900 Census shows the family living in Nacogdoches County with children from both marriages. They were: John Wesley Hill, Hattie Hill, Carrie Hill, Mamie Hill, Jonathan Turner Fears, Beedie Fears and Christopher Columbus Fears.

AUGUSTUS (GUS) FEARS and ROXIE BURK HILL
Married February 10, 1893 in Nacogdoches (Nacogdoches) Texas

1 Augusta
    b. c1857   p. Appleby (Nacogdoches) Texas
    d. 17 Oct. 19   p. Appleby (Nacogdoches) Texas
    b. 1895   p. Nacogdoches, Texas
2. Jonathan Turner
    b. 5 March 1896   p. Appleby (Nacogdoches) Texas
    d. 9 March 1981   p. Lufkin (Angelina) Texas
    b. March 1981   p. Lufkin, Texas (Cedar Grove)
3. Beedie Fitzanna
    b. December 1898   p. Appleby (Nacogdoches) Texas
    d. 4 Dec 1979   p. Houston (Harris) Texas

Augustus (Gus) Fears and Roxie Burk Hill   Jonathan Turner and Beedie Fitzanna
Children of Augustus Fears and Roxie Fears

b. 5 March 1896   p. Appleby (Nacogdoches) Texas
d. 9 March 1981   p. Lufkin (Angelina) Texas
b. 14 March 1981   p. Lufkin, TX (Cedar Grove Cemetery)

Jonathan Turner (J.T.) Fears was born to Augustus (Gus) Fears and Roxie Burk Fears March 5, 1896 in Appleby (Nacogdoches) Texas. The community Midwife, Feby Crain delivered him. The union of Gus and Roxie was the second marriage for each. J. T. was one of three children from this marriage. The family moved to Caro, Texas when Jonathan was age 6.

Jonathan's education training extended to about the 7th grade level, as was typical of the education level provided to Black people in public schools of that period. Learning the basics such as "Reading, Riting and Rithmatic to the Tune of a Hickory Stick" was the method of his day. He often demonstrated his sharp ability of memory and recall to recite the mathematical "times tables" and Anatomy and Physiology lessons of the number of bones in the body and the names of bones in the ear. His favorite poem and his family's favorite were to hear him recite how he learned the alphabets or "ABCs." Each letter of the alphabet was recited as follows: A had an apple pie, B bit it and C cut it, D dove for it, E eyed it, F fought for it, but G got it, H had it, and so on to Z.

Birthplace of Jonathan Turner Fears - Appleby, Texas

JONATHAN TURNER FEARS

J.T.'s music education was provided by his mother Roxie, who with determination and baton raps to sore knuckles, passed to him the few selections he played for his children on the neighbor's, (Mrs. Elvira Bell) piano. In addition to the piano, his mother Roxie owned several musical instruments.

Jonathan Turner Fears was drafted into the U.S. Army, April 1, 1918 at age 22 years during WWI. He trained at Camp Travis, San Antonio, Texas and was shipped to Brest, France via Camp Mill, Long island, N.Y., July 1918. J.T. was hospitalized with pneumonia shortly after arriving in France. Therefore, he missed much of the actual combat. He later served in the Argonne Forest in France where he experienced the so called, "Trench Warfare." After discharge July 12, 1919 at Fort Worth, Texas he returned to Caro, Texas.

J.T.'s story of his call to military service gave an indication of a young man who was enjoying life to the extent that his leaving for basic training was not an adventure that he was anxiously looking forward to. On returning home one evening his mother Roxie ran to meet him crying and in anguish over him having received his draft notice. He said his response to the news was "cold chills and shaking knees and a lump in his throat that he though he would never swallow."

However, being a man who was often down but not out, he went to the draft board the next day to let them know that he could not leave his "poor helpless mother" with no one to take care of her but himself.

Unfortunately his reputation had preceded him. When time came to report to the train station for travel to basic training, he was personally picked up and delivered there by the local sheriff.

The next year or so was spent in training at Camp Travis, San Antonio, Texas and in France with the American Expeditionary Forces, under the command of General John J. "Black Jack" Pershing. General Pershing, during the final push of the American force to defeat the German Army, was said to have stated that it would be "Hell or Hoboken" (N.J.). J.T. became ill with pneumonia in France and was hospitalized until he recovered.

Arriving in Caro via train from Forth Worth, Texas after army discharge, J.T. met his father boarding a train to Nacogdoches, Texas. J.T. continued on to Nacogdoches with him. After his return to Caro and staying there one week, he traveled by train to Humble, Texas to visit his mother. He later returned to Caro. Then, in 1919 he left Caro for Keltys, Texas and began work at the Keltys sawmill where his half-brother, Christopher Fears worked. Jonathan was listed in the 1920 Census in Houston Harris County Texas. Listed with him was his sister Beedie and half-sister Hattie with her daughter Eva. J.T. later met in Keltys, Texas his future wife, Belma.

While living with his brother Christopher Columbus "Lum" Fears, Jonathan T. Fears (J.T.) met Belma Denman who also lived in Keltys. Belma Denman was the daughter of Edmond and Emma Ewing Denman. She had a three-year-old son, Earnest Reese from Elijah Reese. Earnest Reese was born 12 October 1917 in Keltys (Angelina) Texas. Jonathan joined and was baptized at Mount Calvary Baptist Church, Keltys, Texas.

Belma and J. T. married November 23, 1923. J. T., as he recalls the event, rented a house. The morning before leaving for work, he told Belma to cook dinner and he would be back later with a preacher to get married. When he returned with the preacher Belma's hands were full of biscuit dough. She wiped the dough from her hands on her apron and they were joined in marriage. From this union, six children were born: Roxie, Jonathan Turner, Jr., James Denman, Shirley Mae, Johnny Lee and Joel Van.

Roxie was born in Keltys September 17, 1924 in the house shown in the photograph. The family of four left Keltys around 1925/26 and moved to Farmersville, Louisiana. J.T. Fears, Jr. was born there February 28, 1927 and James Fears was born January 20, 1929. During this period, the family moved to Pine Bluff, Arkansas where J.T. worked at the Nash Auto Body plant. He later began working at the Fisher Auto Body plant in Memphis, Tennessee. Belma and the children remained in Pine Bluff.

The family returned to Texas from Pine Bluff 1929 or 1930. Belma and the children, Earnest, Roxie, J.T., Jr. (brother), and James lived with one of her sisters, possibly Veda in Huntington, Texas. For a short time J. T. worked at Zeigler's Mill in Lufkin. In the midst of the depression years the family found it necessary to move again, this time to the oil boomtown of Kilgore, Texas.

Kilgore was a rough oil town. J.T. often told of the famous Texas Ranger, Gonzales who was sent there to enforce law and order. He would relate the story of how his stepson Earnest would throw up silver dollars for Gonzales to shoot. Although J.T. was hopeful that opportunities would be better in this "boom town," the only real treasure that was added to the family was his second daughter Shirley. Shirley was born December 26, 1931 in Kilgore.

Shortly before this happy event took place, the family was preparing for the return to Lufkin.

On December 14, 1931, J. T.'s mother Roxie, for the sum of $250.00 that he gave to her, purchased for him a home at 1501 Paul Ave., Lufkin, Texas. The property did not include electricity nor did it have city provided water. Neither of those necessities was available at that time. This house and land became the final residence for the wandering Fears family. The family returned to Lufkin during the winter of 1932. In 1935 J.T. became ill and was admitted to the Veterans Hospital in Fort Beard, New Mexico. It was during this difficult time that his mother Roxie suffered a stroke at the family residence and died December 10, 1935. Belma was at work. Therefore, as told to the author by his brother James, he, age 6 and Shirley, age 4 were with their grandmother when she was stricken. They told the next-door neighbors, the Shelbys, that "mammaw" is sleeping and that they could not wake her up. Because of J. T.'s illness in New Mexico at a military veteran's hospital, he was not able to attend the funeral. Roxie is buried in the old Post Oak Cemetery North of Nacogdoches, Texas.

These were difficult times for Belma who was now alone with the children. However, some time later that winter, J.T. was released from the hospital and returned to Lufkin. One of the activities that helped to sustain families during the depression years was "moonshining" (Making and selling illegal alcohol), which J.T. engaged in for a while. One amusing incident occurred when Sheriff Luke Langford came to the home to investigate the possible sale of liquor by J.T. When his oldest daughter Roxie and his son J.T., Jr. saw Sheriff Langford approaching the house, Roxie ran to get the bottle and quickly threw the bottle in to the chicken house with such force that the bottle was never found.

Final additions to the family came with the birth of two sons, Johnny Lee on September 25, 1936 and J.V. (Joel Van) on August 10, 1938.

Jonathan T. Fears employed at Texas Foundry

Grave of Jonathan and Belma Denman Fears

b. Dec. 20, 1900	p. Keltys (Angelina) Texas
d. 8 May 1967	p. Lufkin (Angelina) Texas
B. 10 May 1967	p. Lufkin, Cedar Grove, Texas

Children

Belma's first child was Earnest Reese. His father was Elijah Reese.

1. Earnest Reese

b. c1917   p. Keltys (Angelina) Texas

Belma was the third daughter of Edmond Denman and Emma Ewing. Edmond Denman was a sawmill worker/farmer and his wife Emma worked as a maid and cook. Edmond lived near Huntington, Texas in a sawmill community that was known as Odell Creek, Texas. Their daughter, Vada lived and worked there until her move to Lufkin, Texas

Belma's older sister Vada Denman reared Belma and Belma's sister, Eliza "Tige" Denman. Another sister Johnny, the mother of Thelma Moore died at a young age.

Washing, ironing, cooking, babysitting and housekeeping as a maid were many of the jobs Belma held during her lifetime. This propensity for hard work was a characteristic that she encouraged and passed to her children. Washing clothes during her time was done in washtubs with the use of a scrub board. Heavier work clothes were usually washed in a large black iron wash pot with a wood fire burning under it. After washing, the clothes were hung on a clothesline with wooden clothespins. In hot or cold weather, the tasks had to be done, either for her family or her employers.

Belma was well liked by her neighbors and her employers. People who knew her sought numerous times her advice on many issues. Although quiet and unassuming, she was a woman of great courage, strength and determination. She would fiercely defend her children. On an occasion when her daughter saw a man peeping in the window of her house and screamed, she immediately grabbed her husband's Sheriff's model 45 caliber revolver and shot under the window in an attempt to kill the "peeping Tom." Fortunately, the intruder had gone. It was determined later that the "peeper" was someone well known in the community for such an act. The only tine that Belma was absent from her children was after the death her sister Vada.

Belma traveled to Phoenix, Arizona for Vada's funeral. To the relief of her husband and children, she returned home to Lufkin by bus soon after the funeral.

The only fault that Belma exhibited was her refusal to be treated by doctors. Midwives or "grannies" delivered many of her seven children as they were once called. However, the time came when there was no other option than to see a doctor and be committed to the hospital. She suffered kidney failure at a time when kidney dialysis was not available in the Lufkin, Texas area. After finally accepting the need for hospitalization in the Angelina County Memorial Hospital and after several days committed there, she passed into eternity. Belma, a hard working devoted Christian wife and mother will not be forgotten because of the great love that family and friends had for her.

Remembered from the early days was the rear outhouse at 1501 Paul Ave., similar to the one shown below. If outhouses could talk, what a story they could tell.

1. Roxie Fears
   b. September 17, 1924   p. Keltys (Angelina) Texas
   d. September 2, 1977   p. Nacogdoches (Nacogdoches) Texas
   B. September 1977   p. Lufkin, Texas (Davis Memorial Garden)

Roxie, the first born of Jonathan and Belma Fears was born in Keltys (Angelina) Texas, the town of her mother's birth and where her father met and married his mate for life. Roxie was always a girl with an independent mind. By the time that she reached the eleventh grade, she with boldness, announced that she no longer wanted to go to school. Her father, J.T., with all sincerity said, "If you don't go to school, then you will go to work." Roxie was a hard worker and from that day forward, she worked! This was a characteristic that was passed to her from her hard working mother, Belma Fears, who set the pace for all of her children.

She inherited from her grandmother Roxie the same fiery temperament and could "cuss" just as fearsome. After marriage and several children, (one died at birth) work she did! Illness claimed her life at the age of 52. She was a beautiful lady, devoted wife and mother.

ROXIE FEARS AND CURTIS SANDERS
Married 22 August 1942 in Lufkin, Angelina, Texas

Curtis Sanders

b. 1924 to Minnie M. Sanders   p. Carthage, Panola, Texas
d. Date Unknown   p.

Curtis worked hard to provide for his family. The hard work gave him well-developed biceps that his young brother-in-laws, Johnny and J.V. wanted and tried to develop. He worked at other jobs before finally retiring from the Lufkin Paper Mill. J. V. would spend some nights with Roxie and Curtis because they at one time lived near his school, Carver Elementary. Curtis had the desire to improve his education through correspondence courses. He bought the family's first typewriter.

Children: 1. Velma Mae
              b. 7 September 1943   p. Lufkin (Angelina) Texas
Velma M. and (?) Cole
    Barbara Ann Sanders: b. 1959
       Monique Denise Louise Sanders: b. 1983

Daniel Ray Sanders b. 1964
Belinda Sue Davis b. 1968
Tyrone Davis b. 1973

2. Mamie Jean
     b. 23 March 1945   p. Lufkin (Angelina) Texas
     d. 2 June 1996   p. Lufkin (Angelina) Texas
     (Davis Memorial Garden)

Mamie was of gentle nature, very unassuming with a quiet manner. Mamie was the second born living child of Curtis Sanders and Roxie Fears Sanders.

     Mamie Sanders and Jimmy Davis
          1. Sarah Ann Davis b. 1960   d. (?)
          2. Jimmy Davis, Jr. b. 1961
          3. Joel Van Davis: b. 1963

4. Daniel Davis: b. 1964
5. Shelia Davis: b. 1965
6. Diana Kay Davis:
     b. 1966

Mamie Davis with her son Joel (2nd from right). Mamie's sister Renay Sanders (left) and brother, Johnny (right)

3. Curtis Sanders, Jr.
          b. 20 December 1946   p. Lufkin, Angelina, Texas

Roxie and Curtis, having giving birth to two girls, were very likely over joyed at the arrival of their first son, Curtis, Jr.

     Curtis Sanders, Jr. and Lora Hageon
          1. Curtis Sanders: b. 1980
          2. Kurtis Sanders: b. 1982

4. Shirley Fay
          b. 11 February 1949   p. Lufkin, Angelina, Texas
          Shirley Fay and William Earl Taylor
          1. Ronnie Earl: b. 1963
          2. Tony Elbert: b. 1964
          3. William Earl: b. 1966
          4. Sabrina Faye: b. 1967

             Brinda Diane and (?) Coleman
             Shelita Rochelle: b. 1984
             Jamarcus Leon: b. 1985
       5. Aritha Diane: b. 1968
       Marcus Deandre: b. 1984

5. Bonita Gale
        b. 7 June 1951   p. Lufkin (Angelina) Texas

6. Linda Darnell Sanders
        b. 26 July 1953   p. Lufkin (Angelina) Texas
        1. Timothy Sanders: b. 1970
        2. Anthony Sanders: b. 1971
   Linda Sanders and John McElwee
        1. LaSandra McElwee: b. 1974
        2. Diana McElwee: b. 1975

Shown from left to right:
Timothy, LaSandra, Anthony, Linda, and
Diana

7. Patrick Ervin
> b. 22 May 1957   p. Lufkin (Angelina) Texas

Patrick and Barbara McFarland Sanders

Roxie and Christopher
Thyrone Ringer 2/2/2006

1. Roxie Diana Sanders b. 8/28/1982 (Second from left, back row)
2. Kimberly Desiree Sanders b. 7/1/1984 (Third left)
3. Amber Catrice Sanders b. 4/27/1986 (Front row right)
4. Patrick Adams Sanders b. 7/12/1988 (Front row left)
5. Joshua Jared and Jonathan Jeremiah Sanders b. 8/17/90 (Not shown)

8. Johnny Earl
> b. 19 May 1963   p. Lufkin (Angelina) Texas

9. Yolanda Rene
> b. 30 September 1965   p. Lufkin (Angelina) Texas
> 1. Ptolemy Antwan Sexton
>   b. 28 Jan1984   p. Lufkin (Angelina) Texas
> 2. Crystal Jeannette Brown
>   b. 1987   p. Lufkin (Angelina) County
> 3. Freddick Olphant
>   b. 1992   p. Lufkin (Angelina) County

2. Jonathan Turner, Fears Jr.
        b. 28 Feb 1928   p. Farmersville (Union Parish) Louisiana
        d. 24 Jan 1984   p. Houston (Harris} Texas
        B. 24 Jan 1984   p. Houston, TX (Houston Mem. Gardens)

Jonathan (J.T., Jr.) or "Brother," so called by his siblings, was always a partner in "devilishness" with his sister Roxie. They were also their father's chief agents in helping to hide his "bootleg" liquor. Maybe that is why as they grew older they decided to drink their share of it, though thankfully, never becoming alcoholics.

Brother was a hard worker that seemed to take pride in his efforts. He was sincere in his desire to provide for his family, a likely trait that he inherited from his father J.T. However, his marriages were more of a challenge.

JONATHAN TURNER FEARS, JR. AND VELMA HUNTER
Married 1945 in Lufkin, Angelina, Texas

Jonathan, Jr.'s first marriage was to Velma Hunter, from whom he fathered two children, Betty Jean and Charles Edward Fears. It was interesting and somewhat comical to see approaching Jonathan's father's house, Jonathan, Jr., and Velma Hunter, followed by Velma's mother, Dora Hunter with a stick in her hand, held in a threatening manner. She, with the stick in hand, and a stern look on her face, loudly announced that J. T. had gotten her daughter "in a family way" (pregnant) and he was going to marry her. The marriage happened after all official documents were obtained, on the porch of the home of his father and mother, Jonathan Fears, Sr. and Belma Fears, where they lived for a short while until renting a mill house in what was known as the Nesbit Quarters (sawmill quarters). Mill houses or "shotgun houses" were small houses built straight through with a living room bedroom and kitchen. The houses were usually heated with a kerosene or wood stove. They were called shotgun houses because a shotgun fired while standing on the front porch would allow the bullets to go straight through the front entrance and out the back entrance without hitting anything.

Velma Hunter: 28 Jan 1928
    1. Betty Jean Fears
            b. 15 Nov 1945   p. Lufkin, Texas
            d. 6 Mar 2014   p. Houston, Texas
            B. Houston National Cemetery 10410 Veterans Memorial Drive

Betty and J.T. Fears   Betty and Robert

Betty Fears and Ford Lynn Jennings

1. Cynora Faye Jennings Carrier

2. Amahad Rashad Jennings

Betty Jennings and Veazie
3. Robert LeChae Veazie

2. Charles Edward Fears
        b. 25 August 1946   p. Lufkin, Texas

Jonathan Turner Fears' second marriage was to Lillie Mae Grant. Lillie Mae had a son by the name of Eddie Lee Grant.

Jonathan, Jr.'s third marriage was to Lizzie Pearl. A daughter Kathleen was born of this union.

J.T. Jr. moved to Houston, Texas where he was employed for several years.

3. James Denman Fears
    b. 20 Jan. 1929   p. Farmersville (Union Parish) Louisiana

James was a popular student and athlete at Dunbar High School, Lufkin, Texas.

His football playing was put on hold after a fractured leg during a game in 1944, in Longview, Texas. His athletic coach was Coach Smith and later Clarence Franklin, who coached and taught for many years at Dunbar.

James attended Prairie View A&M College but withdrew after marriage to Billie Jean Scott. He began work at the Texas Foundry in Lufkin, Texas and worked there until his retirement. His work there included drafting, sign printing and artist. During his employment with the Texas Foundry he also worked part time wallpaper hanging, sign printing, and miscellaneous work. Much of his additional work was for Mrs. Stigall who kept him busy with her rental houses and with her home until her death.

James Fears' first marriage was to Billy Jean Scott of Camden, Texas. James' marriage to Billy Jean Scott produced three children: James, Jr. (Jimmy), Gilbert Wayne, and Broderick Jacque. His son Broderick (Rickie) is deceased and sons James, Jr. and Gilbert are living in Los Angeles, California, where their mother Billy once lived.

JAMES MARRIED BILLIE JEAN SCOTT IN CAMDEN, TEXAS
September 1949

Billie Jean Scott
    b. 29 Sept. 1933   p. Camden, Texas

1. James Denman, Jr.
        b. 25 April 1950   p. Lufkin (Angelina) Texas

2. Gilbert Wayne
        b. 29 May 1951   p. Lufkin (Angelina) Texas

3. Broderick Jacque
        b. 20 January 1957   p. Lufkin (Angelina) Texas
        d. 3 August 2001   p. Los Angeles, California

JAMES AND JANIE WASHINGTON
Married 1956

James' second marriage was to Janie Washington, her second marriage. Janie's father was a poultry farmer that lived on a farm west of Lufkin, Texas. There were no children born of this marriage. However, Janie had children from her marriage to her first husband J.T. Washington.

JAMES DENMAN FEARS AND DORIS EVANS AMIE
Married 14 April 1973 in Lufkin, Angelina, Texas

Doris Evans Amie
       b. 9 September 1945   p. Chester, Texas
Son - Anthony Amie
       b. 6 August 1966- (Father - Grover Amie)
1. Jerry Lee Fears
       b. 26 August 1974   p. Lufkin (Angelina, Texas

2. Jonathan Tyren Fears
       b. 20 June 1978   p. Lufkin (Angelina) Texas

James' fourth marriage was to Doris Evans Amie. James met Doris who was living with his mother's cousins, Georgia Lee and Sarah. Doris had one son Anthony from Grover Amie, Doris' former schoolmate at Dunbar High School, Lufkin, Texas.

4. Shirley Mae Fears
   b. 26 December 1931   p. Kilgore (Gregg) Texas

Shirley, the baby girl of the Fears family, with a quick temperament in her young days, possibly inherited from her grandmother, Roxie Burk Fears, was smart and very well liked. Shirley, a very caring person always looked after her younger brothers, J.V. and Johnny and relinquished her paper deliverer job to them after she graduated from Dunbar High School and enrolled at Prairie View A&M College, Prairie View, Texas. It was there that she met her first real love, Buford, a star football player. Unfortunately, he died after graduating and enlisting from the ROTC into the U. S. Army.

Shirley was protective of her younger brothers, J. V. and Johnny. She was the big sister that "broke up" the occasional fights and insisted that they always washed their faces and underarms. Of course, the underarm part never quite met her complete approval. Shirley had attractive classmates that would visit her to the delight of her younger brothers. A most frequent visitor was Betty Engram, who to this day is considered as one of her closes friends. They were both members of Long's Chapel CME Church, located on Lining Street in Lufkin, Texas, not far from where they lived.

Shirley, an attractive young lady, had many male admirers. One of those admirers was C. A. Mark, a stoutly built young man from a reasonable well-to-do family was always persistent but never quite successful. C. A. was a close friend of her brother James. Shirley, however did meet that one Prairie View classmate that was not a star athlete or man of imposing stature, but likable, personable and intelligent. Milbrew Davis was the man on the scene at the right place and at the right time. Milbrew was the "bridge over troubled waters" that helped Shirley to overcome the loss of someone (Buford) that she had cared for dearly. Her very protective brothers, J. V. and Johnny who felt that anyone who had an interest in their little sister, certainly had to meet their approval, immediately accepted Milbrew into their family. Milbrew, born in LaGrange, Texas, was the eighth child of George and Victoria Davis of LaGrange, Texas.

After graduation from Prairie View A&M, Milbrew moved from Reserve Officer Training Candidacy to 2nd Lieutenant in the U. S. Army and was transferred to South Korea until called home after learning of the death of his and Shirley's first born son, Milbrew Davis, Jr.

Shirley met Milbrew Davis of LaGrange, Texas while both were students at Prairie View A&M College, Prairie View, Texas. Shirley married Milbrew as a 2nd Lieutenant in the U.S. Army from the ROTC at Prairie View. Milbrew and Shirley married at Long's Chapel CME Church in Lufkin, Texas July 25, 1953, where she was a member, Rev. Blount officiating.

Shirley Mae Fears

b. 26 December 1931   p. Kilgore, Gregg, Texas

SHIRLEY MAE FEARS AND THE REV. DR. MILBREW DAVIS

Left to right:
Charles
Sabrina
Milbrew
Shirley
Tammy

Milbrew Davis

b. 4 November 1930   p. LaGrange, Fayette, Texas

From the union of Milbrew Davis and Shirley Fears were born the following children:
1. Milbrew Davis, Jr.: Died at Birth

b. 1954   p. Lufkin (Angelina) Texas

d. 1954   p. Lufkin (Angelina) Texas

2. Charles James Davis

b. 27 May 1956

p. Austin, Travis, Texas

Charles Davis and Michelle Haward
Children:
1. Candace Davis

2. Charlette Davis

3. Sabrina Joy

      b. 9 April 1960   p. San Antonio (Bexar) Texas

4. Tammy Joyce

      b. 19 July 1967   p. San Antonio (Bexar) Texas

Milbrew and Shirley Davis after the funeral of J.T. Fears, Sr. (Left of Charles is his wife Michelle)
Far left of the family is Charles Fears

5. Johnny Lee Fears

b. 25 Sept. 1936   p. Lufkin, Texas

d. 21 December 1999   p. Dallas (Dallas) Texas

Int: 30 December 1999   p. Dallas, Texas   (Laurel Land Memorial Park)

(Marsalis Ave. Church of Christ)   Sect. Psalms, Block C, Lot 5, Space 1

Johnnie was the fifth child of Belma Fears and J. T. Fears. He was born nearly five years after his sister Shirley. Johnnie stammered or stuttered during his early years. One amusing incident occurred when his sister Roxie gave birth to her first child, Velma. It was Johnnie's first day of beginning school at Carver Elementary.

He was told to go tell His Aunt Veda Matthews that Roxie had given birth. On arriving at his Aunt's home he excitedly attempted to announce to Aunt Veda the important news. However, after several attempts to reveal the exciting news, he finally loudly exclaimed: "Otie (Roxie) had a baby!" No one ever let him forget that excited morning.

Johnnie completed Carver Elementary and later a graduated from Dunbar High School, Lufkin, Texas. Shortly after graduation, he enlisted in the U.S. Navy and completed "Boot Camp" at the U.S. Navy Training Center, San Diego, California. His first assignment was at the Naval Air Station, Jacksonville, Florida where he served as an aircrew member on naval aircrafts and aboard the Navy's first Super Aircraft Carriers, the USS Forrestal and later, the USS Saratoga.

After release from active duty, Johnny retuned to Lufkin, Texas. Lack of a job opportunity and boredom led to his reenlistment in the Navy. His first enlistment was served in the Atlantic and Mediterranean areas, but his second enlistment led to the opposite side of the world. He was stationed in California and lastly, the Naval Air Station Agana, Guam.

It was there that he became ill from a kidney disorder. After transfer to San Diego, California, one of his kidneys was removed. After a period of recovery, Johnnie was allowed to return home on leave. Johnnie continued his service in the Navy after his recovery until his discharge 6 September 1963.

Johnnie returned to Lufkin after discharged from the U.S, Navy. He was employed at the Texas Foundry where his brother James and his father J.T. were also employed. In belief that employment opportunities would be better, he moved from Lufkin to Houston, Texas and was employed there where his brother J.T., Jr. worked.

After returning to Lufkin, Johnnie married Joyce Simmons who had a daughter, Carla Simmons in Lufkin, Texas. From Joyce, Johnny fathered two sons: Victor L. Fears, December 28, 1968 and Julius T. Fears, December 28, 1969.

Johnnie later moved to Dallas, Texas, where after divorce from Joyce, he married Helen Davis. His Nephew Charles Fears was also residing in Dallas.

The one kidney that Johnny had after the first was removed while in the U.S. Navy, also began to fail requiring him to be placed on kidney dialysis. After repeated hospitalizations, Johnny passed December 21, 1999. His funeral service was held December 30, 1999 at Marsalis Avenue Church of Christ, Dallas, Texas.

Note:

An image of Johnny's Death Certificate is on page 72.

JOHNNY FEARS AND JOYCE HARDY SIMMONS
Married1968 in Lufkin, Texas

Johnny and Joyce Simmons
    1. Victor Lamar
        b. 28 December 1968   p. Lufkin, Texas

    2. Julius T.
        b. 28 December 1969   p. Lufkin, Texas

Julius Fears with his children
and a daughter are from his former wife Dawn N. Bell

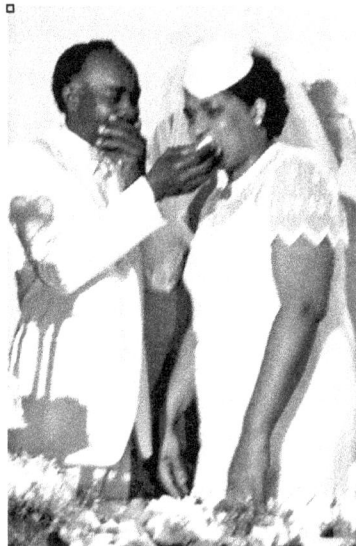

JOHNNIE AND HELEN CHRISTMAN DAVIS
Dallas, Texas

6. Joel Van Fears

b. 10 August 1938   p. Lufkin, Angelina, Texas

Joel Van Fears was the youngest and 6th child of Jonathan Turner and Belma Fears. He was born, reared and received his early education in Lufkin, Texas. Joel attended Carver Elementary School and graduated from Dunbar Junior Senior High in 1956. His football playing for Dunbar ended after receiving a fractured clavicle during a game in Longview, Texas. Joel graduated as an honor student from Dunbar.

Joel's birth name was "J. V." The name was from his mother's cousin who was referred to by the name J.V. Penson, although his full name was Joseph V. Penson. Prior to enlistment in the U. S. Navy, he changed his name to Joel, a name suggested by his sister Shirley.

Joel entered military service in June of 1956 for three years in the U.S. Navy and received basic training at the Naval Training Center in San Diego, California. After basic training, Joel was assigned to temporary duty at North Island Naval Air Station in San Diego, California. Thereafter, he received training at the Navy's aviation preparation school in Norman, Oklahoma and Air Controlman Airborne Early Warning training at NAS Glyncoe, Brunswick, Georgia. Joel was assigned to duty at NAS Agana, Guam with Airborne Early Warning Squadron 1 (VW-1) from June 1957 until 1958 and was released from active duty in 1959 as a Petty Officer 2nd Class.

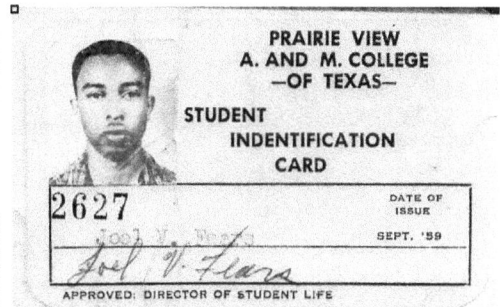

Joel prepared for a lifetime career as an engineer at Prairie View A & M College, Prairie View, Texas. He received a Bachelor of Science degree in electrical engineering in January 1965. After graduation Joel moved to Florida and was employed by NASA (National Aeronautics and Space Administration) at the John F. Kennedy Space Center (Merritt Island Launch Area) for 11 months before transferring to Manned Space Center (Johnson Space Center), Houston, Texas. After one year and 10 months service there he returned to the Kennedy Space Center in Florida, October 1967.

This move resulted from his marriage to Mary L. Jackson Anderson July 21, 1967 in Sanford, Seminole County, Florida. Mary, a divorced mother of two children, John H. Anderson, Jr. and Julie L. Anderson, lived in Daytona Beach, Florida where the couple resides.

Joel joined Stewart Memorial United Methodist Church within two months after relocating to Daytona Beach. He has held several offices in his church, District and Conference United Methodist Church. He served as Scoutmaster and Cub Master at Stewart Memorial for 21 years. Joel was President of the DeLand District United Methodist men for two years and was elected Lay Leader of the DeLand District United Methodist Church. He continues to serve in the East Central District and in the Florida Conference.

Joel retired March 31, 1995 after 30 years of employment with NASA. Afterwards, he worked at Daytona Beach Community College for three years as Coordinator of a Federal grant for minority students. He was introduced at his Retirement Luncheon in Daytona Beach, Florida July 29, l995 as "The Man From Texas."

Joel participates with his wife Mary in Civil War Reenactments in Florida primarily, and occasionally in other states. Joel, Mary and son John H. Anderson, Jr. perform together and sometimes Joel. Jr. performs also.

Mary Luvenia Jackson
b. April 3, 1930   p. Pelham (Cotton), Mitchell, Georgia
Mary is a graduate of Crooms Academy High School, Sanford, Florida, Bethune-Cookman College (Now Bethune-Cookman University) Daytona Beach, Florida with a BS Degree in Secondary Education with a Major in Business Education, and a Master of Science Degree from the School of Library Science Florida State University. Mary worked in schools in Georgia and Florida. She retired as an Elementary School Media Specialist from Westside Elementary School in 1986. After retirement, Mary authored four books, The Jackson – Moore Family History and Genealogy, Slave Ancestral Research It's Something Else, Civil War and Living History Reenacting About People of Color. Julie's Journey, a story of the last 10 years of Julie's life. An additional book, The Memoir of A Re-enactor of Voices From The Past: The "People of Color" In The Civil War has been authored and is ready for publication.

Mary is a professional storyteller and Civil War Re-enactor. Her storytelling began while employed as an elementary school media specialist. She became interested in Civil War re-enacting when she and husband Joel visited an annual Civil War re-enactment near Lake City, FL in February 2001 called the "Battle of Olustee."

This resulted from a question from a Black Civil War re-enactor as to why black people were not attending the event. Her reply was, "I will see about that."

At the next meeting of the Afro-American Historical and Genealogical Society, Central Florida Chapter, the suggestion was made that the chapter should consider presenting at the event. The chapter made its first presentation at Olustee February 2002.

1. Joel V. Fears, Jr.

b. 5 August 1973   p. Daytona Beach, Volusia, Florida

Joel, Jr. is a Licensed Massage Therapist and has a BS Degree in Alternative Medicine. He received Massage Therapist training at Daytona Beach Community College and his Bachelor of Science Degree from Everglades University, Maitland, Florida.

Joel V. Fears, Jr. is the first and only child of Joel V. Fears and the third child of Mary Fears.

Mary's first two children were John H. Anderson, Jr. and Julie LaVera Anderson (deceased) from her first marriage to John H. Anderson, Sr. (deceased). John has degrees in Music and Chemistry. Julie earned a degree in Fashion Merchandizing. However, she worked for Dean Witter as an Investment Counselor. Both were graduates of Florida State University.

Joel, Sr. in Scoutmaster uniform
and Joel, Jr. (Abt. Age 2)

b. 8 Dec 1898   p. Appleby (Nacogdoches) Texas
d. 4 Dec 1977   p. Houston (Harris) Texas

BEEDIE F. FEARS and WILL MCDANIEL
Married Nacogdoches (Nacogdoches) Texas

BEEDIE FEARS and FREDDIE BRAZOS
Married in Nacogdoches, Texas

1. Freddie Beedie
   b. 25 Oct 1925   p. Houston (Harris) Texas
2. Frankie
   b. 20 Dec 1927   p. Houston (Harris) Texas
   d. 3 Sep 1999   P. Houston (Harris) Texas
3. Ida Mae
   b. 20 Dec 1927   p. Houston (Harris) Texas
4. Anna Jean
   b. 30 May 1935   p. Houston (Harris) Texas
5. Beedie LaVern.
   b. 9 August 1938   p. Houston (Harris) Texas

Frank Brazos
(Little Brother)

Children of Jonathan T. Fears, Sr. and Beedie Fears Brazos
Left to Right: Joel "J.V." Fears, James Fears, Ida Brazos McLemore, Beedie Brazos, Johnny Fears,
Shirley Fears Davis and Anna Jean Brazos Curtis
(Taken after the funeral of J.T. Fears, Jr.

CAROLINE (CALLIE) FEARS
Second child of Beedie Long Fears

CAROLINE FEARS and WILLIS CRAWFORD
Married in Nacogdoches, Texas

1. Lillie
    b. March 25, 1903   p. Nacogdoches, Texas
    d. May 6, 1945

BEEDIE (WEAVER) FEARS

BEEDIE (WEAVER) FEARS and TOM FEARS
Married c1863 Nacogdoches, Texas

Tom Fears
    b. c1829
    p. Georgia
    d. Feb. 17, 1912
    p. Nacogdoches (Nacogdoches) Texas

1. Wiley
        b. c1864   p. Nacogdoches (Nacogdoches) Texas
2. Doc
        b. c1867   p. Nacogdoches (Nacogdoches) Texas
3. Ida B.
        b. c1869   p. Nacogdoches (Nacogdoches) Texas
4. Hattie
        b. c1872   p. Nacogdoches (Nacogdoches) Texas
5. William Noble
        b. c1874   p.
6   Mony (James?)
        b. c1878   p.

WYLIE FEARS

Wylie Fears and Alice

1. Enos
   b. Nacogdoches (Nacogdoches) Texas
   d. Unknown

2. Amos
   b. Nacogdoches (Nacogdoches) Texas
   d. Unknown

DOC FEARS

IDA B. FEARS

HATTIE FEARS

WILLIAM NOBLE "Nobe" FEARS

William Noble Fears was one most often talked about by Jonathan Turner Fears, who referred to him as "Uncle Nobe." Noble was a schoolteacher who taught Jonathan. William Noble later earned a law diploma through correspondence. Noble had a child, Maudie from Lulu Bolden. James, Clytie, Avis and Mildred were Children from Minnie Wilson.

WILLIAM NOBLE FEARS AND LULU BOLDEN
Married Nacogdoches, Texas

2. Maudie
   b.   p. Nacogdoches (Nacogdoches) Texas
   d. May 1982   p. Galveston, Texas

WILLIAM NOBLE FEARS AND MINNIE WILSON
Married 1910 Keltys, Texas

William Noble Fears	Minnie Mae Wilson
b. 1874	b. 8 Oct 1890
p. Nacogdoches, Nacogdoches, Texas	p. Keltys (Angelina) Texas
d. 191?	d. 9 Jan 1986
p. Lufkin, Texas	p. Baton Rouge, Louisiana

Children

3. James
   b. 7 September 1906   p. Keltys (Angelina) Texas
   d. 22 October 1989   p. Dallas, Texas

4. Clytie
   b. 29 September 1911   p. Keltys (Angelina) Texas
   d.   p. Baton Rouge, Louisiana

5. Avis
   b. 04 October 1913   p. Keltys (Angelina) Texas
   d. 30 January 1988   p. Alexandria, Louisiana

6. Mildred
   b. 30 August 1915   p. Lufkin (Angelina) Texas
   d.   p.

MONEY (James?)

VINEY THORN (Thorne)

Viney Thorn
          b. Circa 1840   p. Tillis Ford Stern or Mayo, Texas
          d. 31 October 1914   p. Nacogdoches, Texas

Viney Thorn is the oldest confirmed ancestor on Jonathan Turner Fears' maternal (mother) side of his family. Viney who is believed to be of Indian (Cherokee) descent, was born about 1840 near Stern or Mayo, Texas in Nacogdoches County? Although it is not known who her parents were, she had a half brother.

Abe Sutphen married Viney Thorn in 1851. This union produced 12 children: Francis, b. 1852; Ann, b. 1856; Rosie Adaline, b. 1859; John, b. 1858; Abe b. 1863; Rufus, b. 1866; William, b. 1872; Albert, born 1873; Enoch, b. 1875; Dock Sidney, b. 1878; Sie (Sy), b. 1879, and Arthur, b. 27 Dec 1883, Abe died in 1910, and Viney was last recorded living with her son, Will in the 1910 Census of Nacogdoches County.

VINEY THORN AND JOHN BURK

John Burk (Caucasian)
          b.   p. South Carolina
          d.   p. Nacogdoches (Nacogdoches) Texas
          b.   p. Nacogdoches (Nacogdoches) Texas

1. Roxie Burk
          b. 1859   p. Douglass (Nacogdoches) Texas
          d. 1935   p. Lufkin (Angelina) Texas
          Buried Nacogdoches, Texas in Old North Church Cemetery
2. John Burk
          b. 1860   p. Douglass (Nacogdoches) Texas
          d.   p.

Roxie was with her parents on Galveston Island, Texas when Union General Gordon Granger came ashore and declared all slaves in Texas forever free. (See page 14)

ROXIE BURK AND ELI HILL
Married 27 December 1874

1. Emily
   b.   p. Galveston Texas
   d.   p.
2. John
   b.   P. Galveston, Texas
   d.   p. Lufkin, Texas
3. Vina
   b. 16 August 1877   p. Galveston, Texas
   d. 04 February 1908   p.
   B. Old North Church   p. Nacogdoches, Texas
4. Hattie
   b.   p. Galveston, Texas
   d.   p. Lufkin, Texas
   B. Old North Church   p. Nacogdoches, Texas
5. Carrie
   b.   p. Galveston, Texas
   d.
6. Mamie Hill Ross
   b.   p. Galveston, Texas
   d.   p. Texas
   B Old North Church   p. Nacogdoches, Texas
7. Sarah Hill Aldridge
   b. June 1892   p. Galveston, Texas
   d. October 20, 1950   p. Woodville, Texas
   B.   p. Nacogdoches, Texas

Mamie Hill Ross

VINA HILL AND JOHN FRAILEY
Married 13 August 1892
Rev. J. G. Greer

John Frailey
b. 16 August 1879

d. 04 February 1908

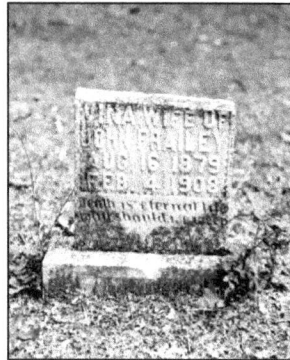

1. Roxanna Frailey
b. October 1896

2. Emma Frailey
b. June 1893

3. Leroy Frailey
b. August 1898

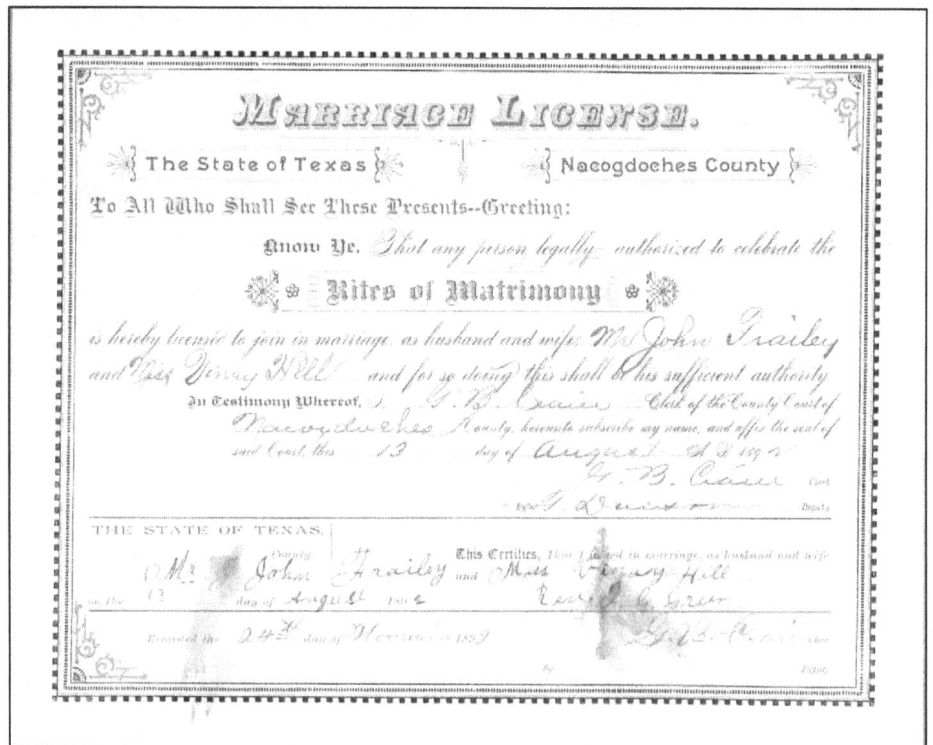

VINEY THORN b. c1840 AND ABE SUTPHEN b. ca 1820
Married 1851 Nacogdoches, Texas

Children
1. Frances
        b. 1852
2. Ann
        b. 1856
4. John
        b. 1858
3. Rosie Adaline
        b. 1859
5. Abron or Abe
        b. 1863
        d. 1910
6. Rufus
        b. 1866
        d. 6 Mar 1920 (Ref. Fredia Sutphen Thomas – (Dallas, Texas)
7. William
        b. 1872
8. Albert
        b. 1873
9. Enoch
        b. 1875
10. Dock Sidney
        b. January 1878
        d. 9 Sept 1925
11. Sie
        b. 1879
        d. 1936
12. Arthur
        b. 27 Dec 1883

DOCK SUTPHEN AND NETTIE B. CRAIN
Married 1899 Nacogdoches, Texas

1. A. B.
      b. April 1900   p. Nacogdoches (Nacogdoches) Texas
      d.
2 Abron
      b. April 1900   p. Nacogdoches (Nacogdoches) Texas
      d. March 20, 1985   p. Nacogdoches (Nacogdoches) Texas
3. Hattie
      b. July 27, 1905   p. Nacogdoches (Nacogdoches) Texas
      d. May 21,1973   p. Lufkin (Angelina) Texas
      br. May 23, 1973   p. North Redland Cemetery, Nacogdoches, Texas

DOCK SUTPHEN AND POLLY SUTPHEN

1. Dock Sutphen
      b. May 15, 1915   p. Texas
      d. August 13, 1974   p. Houston (Harris)Texas
      br. August 18, 1974   p. North Redland Cemetery, Nacogdoches, Texas

Dock Sutphen

2. Sy Sutphen

3. Authur Sutphen

4. Albert Sutphen

5. Ruth Sutphen

ALEX AND LECIE DENMAN
Married c1855 Angelina County, Texas

ALEX DENMAN
>   b.   d.
>   p. Georgia   p. Huntington, Texas

1. John
>   b. c1856
>   d.

2. Jack
>   b. c1860
>   d.

3. *Sarah
>   b. c1864
>   d.

4. Alex
>   b. c1868
>   d.

5. Edmond
>   b. 1870 Angelina County, Texas
>   d.

6. Francis
>   b. Angelina County, Texas
>   d.

*SARAH DENMAN TOWNSEND

Sarah is listed in the 1900 Census with her husband John Townsend and son Monroe. Her daughter Georgia is listed in the same census as married to Napoleon Lee with two of their children, a son Curtis and daughter Elmer. Two additional children, a son Napoleon, Jr. and daughter Sarah were listed in the 1910 Census.

NOTE:

Ancestors born before 1865 were slaves.

EDMOND DENMAN AND EMMA EWING
Married January 18, 1893, Lufkin Angelina Texas

As Texas was settled, many of its inhabitants were from various locations throughout the South. Accompanying these early pioneers were their chattel, those who had been slaves of these families for generations. Such was the history of the parents and grandparents of Edmond Denman (Denmon) and Emma Ewing Denman.

Edmond was born in Angelina County, May 1870, only five years after his parents were freed from slavery. Edmond was the sixth child of Alex and Lecie Denman, their third child to be born in freedom. The 1870 Census revealed that Alex and Lecie were both born in Georgia and with them were children John, Jack, Sarah, Alex, and Edmond. Another daughter, Francis (Frank) was not listed until the 1880 census.

Edmond and Emma were married in November 1893. From this union were born 5 children, one son and 4 daughters: Vada, Eliza, Belma, Frank (a boy), and Johnnie Fae.

Emma and Edmond Denman

Children:
VADA Denman Matthews
Born c1896
Odell Creek, Texas
Died 19 May 1951
Phoenix, Arizona

ELIZA Denman Higgs (Aunt Tige)
Born c1898
Keltys, Texas
Died: 19
Phoenix, Arizona

BELMA Denman
Born 15 Dec 1900
Keltys, Texas

FRANK Denman
Born Keltys, Texas

JOHNNIE Fae Denman Moore
Born Keltys, Texas

Thelma Lerlean Moore daughter of Johnnie
Fae Moore and Willie Moore
b. 26 Dec 1924 d. 30 Dec 2009
br. 9 Jan 2010

Belma was born December 15, 1900 in Keltys, TX. Belma Denman had one son, Earnest born in 1917 from Elijah Reese. Belma married Jonathan Turner Fears in 1923 in Keltys (Angelina) Texas and gave birth to children Roxie, Jonathan, Jr., James, Shirley, Johnny, and Joel V. Belma, until her death in 1967, lived at 1501 Paul Ave Lufkin, Texas.

EARNEST REESE

Earnest Reese was born 1917 in Keltys, Texas.

Earnest Reese was the first born of Belma Denman and Elijah Reese.

ROXIE FEARS SANDERS

Roxie was born 1929 in Keltys, Angelina County, Texas

Roxie was the first child born of Jonathan Turner Fears and Belma Denman Fears.

JONATHAN TURNER FEARS, JR.

Jonathan T. Fears was born February 28, 1927 in Farmersville, Union Parrish, Louisiana.

Earnest Reese

JAMES DENMAN FEARS

James D. Fears was born January 21, 1929 in Farmersville, Union Parrish, Louisiana

SHIRLEY MAE FEARS

Shirley M. Fears was born December 26 1931 in Kilgore, Gregg County Texas

JOHNNY FEARS

Johnny Fears was born September 25, 1936 in Lufkin, Angelina County, Texas

JOEL VAN FEARS (J.V.)

Joel V. Fears was born August 10, 1938 in Lufkin, Angelina County, Texas

FRANK DENMAN

JOHNNIE DENMAN

Johnnie Moore married and gave birth to a daughter, Thelma.

Thelma had a daughter Johnny Mae Ray.

FRANCIS DENMAN

Francis Denman Penson is listed in the 1900 Census with her children Joseph V. (J.V.), Monroe, Alex, and Vessie.

MARIAH EWING

SAM EWING AND LAURA

EMMA EWING was born 1874 to Sam and Laura Ewing at Odell Creek, which was near the site of the Ewing Farm. The Ewing farm was located near Huntington (Angelina) Texas. Laura D. Ewing recounts a history of the Ewing family in a book, Our Ewing Family, Copyright c1978 by Spindletop Museum. Sam was born on the Ewing farm. Additional children of Sam and Laura Ewing listed in the 1900 census were Henry, George, Holly, Charles, James, Champ, and Rhoda.

STATE OF TEXAS   **CERTIFICATE OF DEATH**   **STATE FILE NUMBER**

1. NAME OF DECEASED (a) FIRST	(b) MIDDLE	(c) LAST	(d) MAIDEN	2. SEX	3. DATE OF DEATH
Johnnie	Lee	Fears		Male	December 21, 1999

4. DATE OF BIRTH	5. AGE	6. BIRTH PLACE	7. SOCIAL SECURITY NO.
September 25, 1936	63	Lufkin, Texas	459-56-1420

8. RACE			11. EDUCATION
Black			12

12. MARITAL STATUS	13. SURVIVING SPOUSE	14a. OCCUPATION	14b. KIND OF BUSINESS
MARRIED	Helen Christman	Sand Blaster	TXI Industries

15a. RESIDENCE STREET ADDRESS	15b. CITY OR TOWN
4224 Humphrey Drive	Dallas

15c. COUNTY	15d. STATE	15e. ZIP CODE	15f. INSIDE CITY LIMITS
Dallas	Texas	75216	YES

16. FATHER'S NAME	17. MOTHER'S MAIDEN NAME
Jonathan Fears, Sr.	Belma Denman

18. PLACE OF DEATH: HOSPITAL — ER/OUTPATIENT

19. COUNTY OF DEATH	20. CITY OR TOWN	21. NAME OF HOSPITAL OR INSTITUTION
Dallas	Dallas	Methodist Medical Center

22. INFORMANT — NAME & RELATIONSHIP	23. MAILING ADDRESS OF INFORMANT
Helen Fears – wife	4224 Humphrey Dr. Dallas, Texas 75216

Method of Disposition: BURIAL

Laurel Land Memorial Park
Dallas, Texas

Psalms
C
5
1

Dec. 30, 1999

Name & Address of Funeral Home:
Cedar Crest Place
Funeral Home
4830 So. Lancaster
Dallas, Texas 75216

Certifier: MEDICAL EXAMINER — ON THE BASIS OF EXAMINATION AND/OR INVESTIGATION, IN MY OPINION DEATH OCCURRED AT THE TIME, DATE, PLACE, AND DUE TO THE CAUSE(S) AND MANNER AS STATED

	DATE SIGNED			TIME OF DEATH
Medical Examiner	12	22	1999	4:27 P.M

Joni L. McClain, M.D.   P.O. Box 35728   Dallas, Texas 75235-0728

PART I

IMMEDIATE CAUSE: → Arteriosclerotic cardiovascular disease

DUE TO (OR AS A LIKELY CONSEQUENCE OF):

PART II OTHER SIGNIFICANT CONDITIONS: AUTOPSY: NO   AUTOPSY FINDINGS AVAILABLE: NO

DID TOBACCO USE CONTRIBUTE TO DEATH: UNKNOWN

DID ALCOHOL USE CONTRIBUTE TO DEATH: UNKNOWN

WAS DECEDENT PREGNANT: AT TIME OF DEATH: NO   WITHIN LAST 12 MO.: NO

MANNER OF DEATH: NATURAL

DATE RECEIVED BY LOCAL REGISTRAR	SIGNATURE OF LOCAL REGISTRAR
DEC 29 1999	Lynda Jo Humphrey

NOTES

Some original Fears family documents are held in the East Texas Research Center, Nacogdoches, Texas and earlier documents can be found at the Georgia Archives, Atlanta, GA and in the Troup County Archives, LaGrange, GA. Information for writing the Fears history was also found in documents in the Lufkin, Texas Kurth Library Genealogy Department, the City Library and in libraries and archives in Houston, Texas. A brief period of research was done at the Library of Congress in Washington, DC.

Journey's End

From my early youth to the present, I heard many family stories, searched many documents and traveled to many places, far and near in search of my family's history. The journey has been long and was tiring sometimes, but always rewarding and exciting when glittering diamonds of family lore and trinkets of family history were discovered. Hopefully this wealth of knowledge of family history will be cherished for decades to come. My joy is complete.

76

79

Milbrew and Shirley Davis

Milbrew and Shirley Davis – Mary and Joel Fears

Joel V. Fears, Sr. and Mary Fears
47th Anniversary Outing

Curtis Sanders

Roxie Fears Sanders

Yolanda Rene, Mamie Jean, Joel Van and Johnny Earl

Velma Mae Sanders

Curtis Sanders, Jr.

Patrick Sanders

CHARLES J. DAVIS

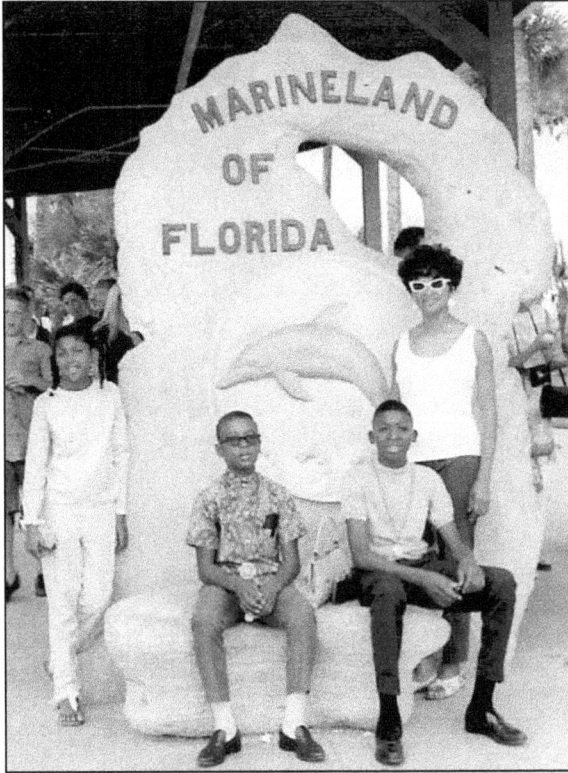

Charles With Aunt Mary and Julie and Andy

Charles Davis With His Daughter Candace

Charles and Michelle With Candace

Charles, Michelle, Charlette and Candace Davis

FEARS FAMILY ALBUM

Charles James Davis

Charles Davis With His Father Milbrew And His Sisters Sabrina and Tammy

Charles and Michelle Davis

Charles Davis With Charlette's Family

84

The Family of Joel Fears, Sr.
FEARS FAMILY ALBUM

JOEL V. FEARS, SR. (J.V.)

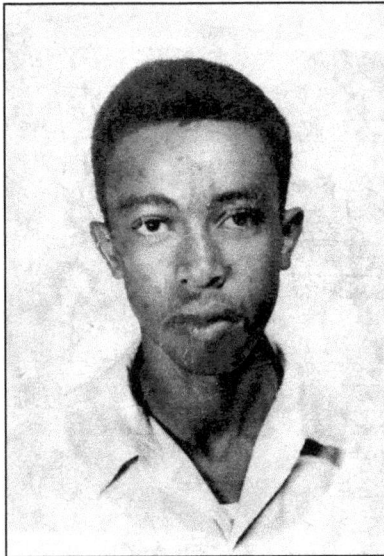

Age 11 Years

Age 16 Years

Age 27 Years

Lufkin, Texas Early Years Downtown

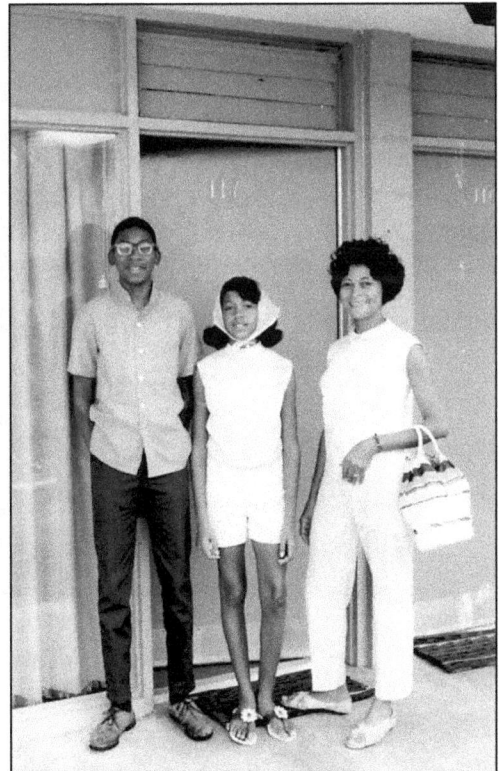

Mobile, Alabama–Andy, Julie and Mary
To Lufkin, Texas

Jewell Jackson, Mary Fears' Mother, Mary and

Dr. Florence Rone. Joel, Jr.'s Godmother
Joel Fears, Jr. (Jody)

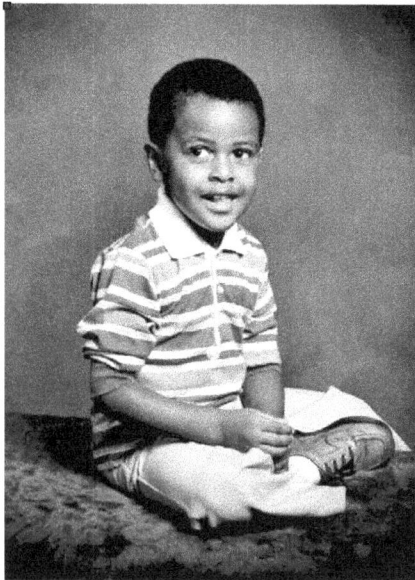

Joel V. Fears, Jr. Age 2 Years

Joel V. Fears, Jr. Age 6 Years

Joel V. Fears, Jr.

Joel V. Fears, Jr. School Soccer

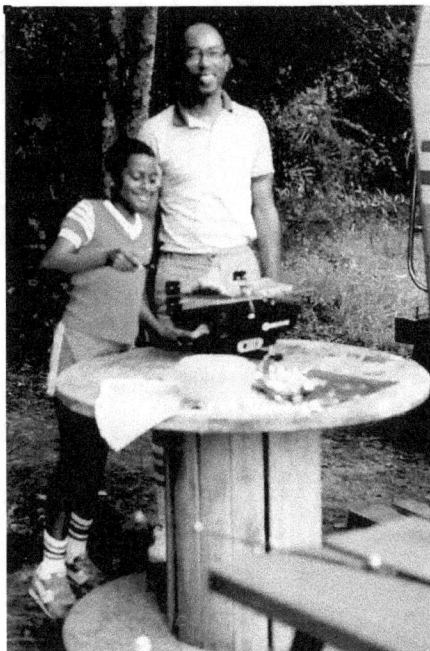

Joel, Sr. and Joel, Jr. RV Camp

Joel V. Fear, Jr., Model Rocket Pilot

Joel V. Fears, Jr., Acrobat

FEARS FAMILY ALBUM

Joel V. Fears, Jr.

Joel Jr. and Joel, Sr. Boy Scout Troop 108

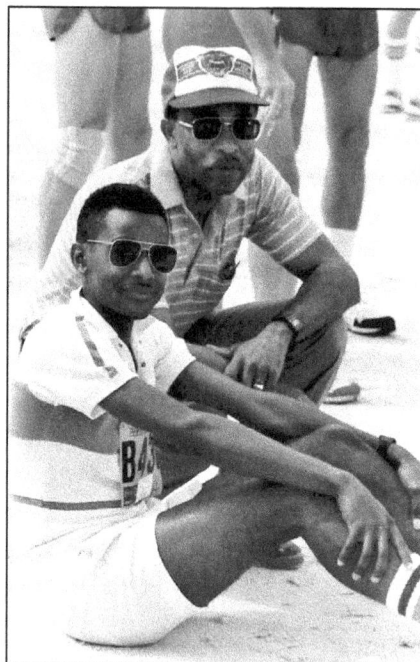

On The Beach 5K Race

Joel, Jr. and Cousin Tammy – San Antonio, TX

Everglades Univ. Graduate

James Denman Fears

James and Doris Fears

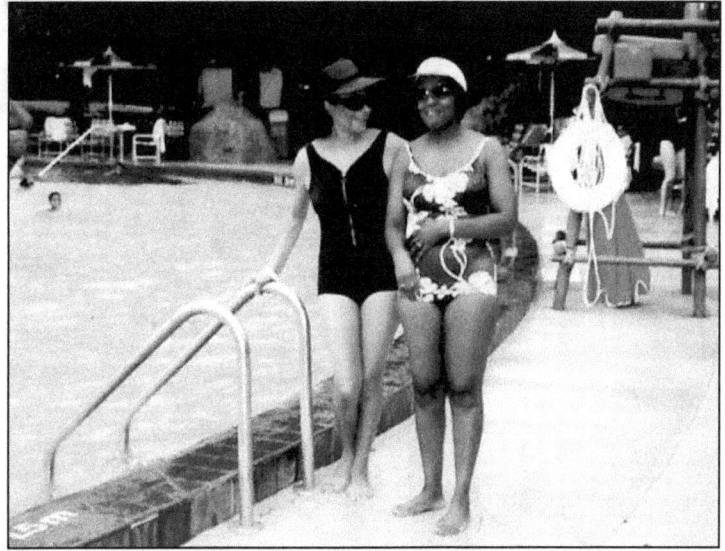

Doris and Mary at Disney World

Johnny, Gilbert and James, Jr.

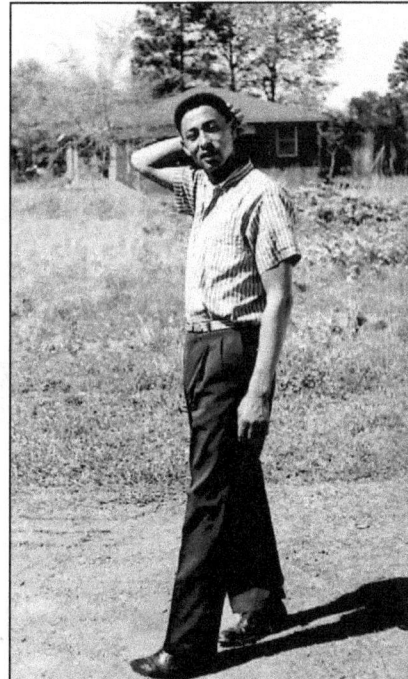

James D. Fears, Sr.

Shirley Fears Davis

Family of Milbrew and Shirley Davis
Nephew Robert Veazie in back center

Fred Brazos (Little Brother) and Shirley Fears Davis

Johnny L. Fears

Julius Fears and Family

Patrick Sanders

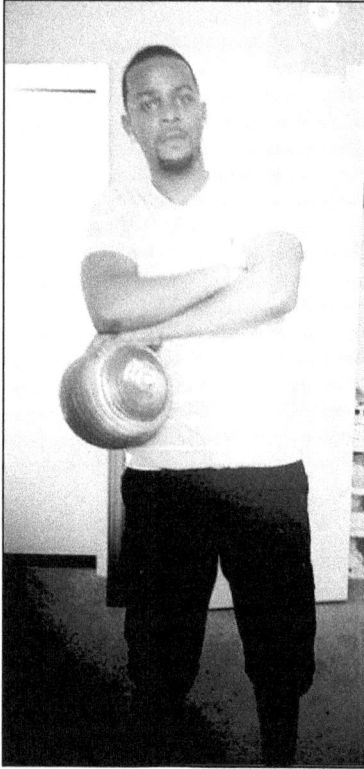

Joshua Jared and Jonathan Jeremiah Sanders

Amber Patrice Sanders

Roxie Sanders Ringer (Left)
Cousin Kimberly Sanders

FEARS FAMILY ALBUM

Joel V. Fears, Jr. (Jody)

Lufkin, Texas - Grandfather Jonathan (J.T.)

Joel, Jr. With Grandfather Sylvester Jackson,
Grandmother Jewell and Joel Sr.

Joel, Jr. with Uncle James
and Grandfather J.T. Fears

FEARS FAMILY ALBUM
Joel V. Fears, Jr.

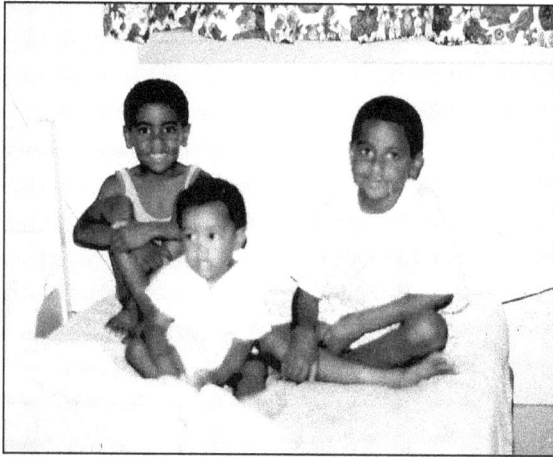

Jerry, Jonathan, Joel, Jr.

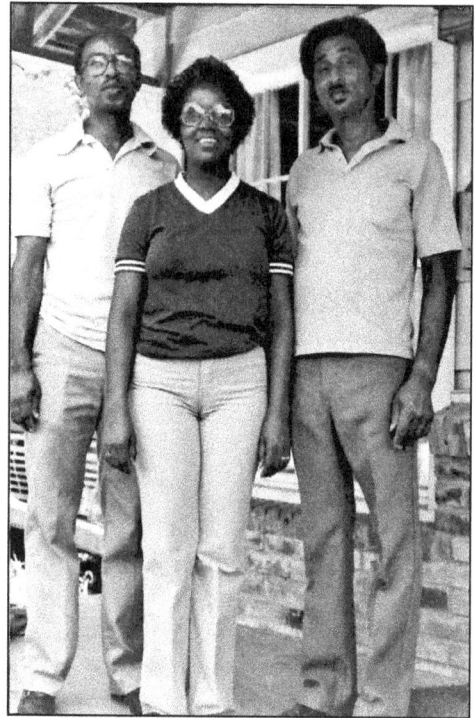

Joel, Sr., Doris and James Fears

Jerry, Jonathan, Joel and James Fears, Sr.

Jerry, Jonathan and Joel, Jr. Lufkin, Texas

Engineer at Kennedy Space Center Office

Author Fears Denman Family History

This family photograph album pictorially represents many different events that involved members of the family over the years of our lives. Hopefully, in years to come our children, grandchildren and all family members will remember and appreciate the efforts and sacrifices that were willingly made to insure that those following us will also have a story to tell of their lives and times.

Augustus and Roxie Fears

Edmond and Emma Denman

www.ingramcontent.com/pod-product-compliance
Lightning Source LLC
Chambersburg PA
CBHW080000280326
41935CB00013B/1700